WHEN CRISIS COMES HOME

Revised and Expanded

Grace & Pearl,

John Geffen

Smyth & Helwys Publishing, Inc.
6316 Peake Road
Macon, Georgia 31210-3960
1-800-747-3016
©2009 by Smyth & Helwys Publishing
All rights reserved.
Printed in the United States of America.

The paper used in this publication meets the minimum requirements of
American National Standard for Information Sciences—
Permanence of Paper for Printed Library Materials.
ANSI Z39.48–1984. (alk. paper)

Library of Congress Cataloging-in-Publication Data

Lepper, M. John.
When crisis comes home / by John Lepper. --[Rev. ed.].
p. cm.
Includes bibliographical references.
ISBN 978-1-57312-539-0
(pbk. : alk. paper)
1. Family--Religious life.
2. Crisis management--Religious aspects--Christianity.
I. Title.
BV4526.3.L47 2009
248.8'6—dc22
2009022958

When

CRISIS

COMES HOME

Revised and Expanded

JOHN LEPPER

Praise for

WHEN CRISIS COMES HOME

When Crisis Comes Home offers a fresh resource for individuals, families, and ministers. Its engaging stories, practical proposals, and readable style are ideal for someone in the midst of a painful situation. When life falls apart, this book can be a helpful starting place for individuals and families.

I found it biblically solid, theologically grounded, and thoughtfully deep. Yet, its readable style touches the core of suffering with extraordinarily functional guidance. Lepper's years of pastoral and counseling experience shine through in his selection of stories, cases, and personal sharing. Throughout the book, his sensitivity, empathy, and wisdom focus on faith, hope, and family love. . . .

I would recommend this book to individuals in crises for their personal comfort, healing, and growth; to seminary students and clergy for their understanding of crisis ministry; to chaplains and counselors for their reflections on cases; and for churches as an excellent resource for study in small groups, support groups, or Bible study.

— G. Wade Rowatt
Professor of Pastoral Care, Baptist Seminary of Kentucky
Clinical Member AAMFT
Diplomate, AAPC
Supervisor, ACPE

When crisis comes home, John Lepper says that we are challenged by hopelessness and meaninglessness. These are powerful forces. This book will help you find perspective that guides, hope that sustains, and insight that informs. I'll keep a copy close by.

— Charles L. Qualls
Associate Pastor for Pastoral Care, Second-Ponce de Leon Baptist Church
Atlanta, Georgia

DEDICATED TO THE MEMORY OF

Merle J. Lepper, Sr.
Neta McCall Lepper
Saidee Bunn Jackson

Who lived and died with an abiding and unwavering faith
in God's love and care.

Who faced crises in their lives by trusting
in the sustaining grace of God.

Who communicated in numerous ways
their belief that nothing can separate us
from the love of God in Jesus Christ.

ACKNOWLEDGMENTS

I am indebted to a number of people for insights and assistance with this book. I would like to thank my wife, Connie, for her invaluable help. She read the manuscript at various stages, offering suggestions for improvement and also meticulously making grammatical corrections. I would also like to thank Connie and our daughters, Allison and Tanya, for allowing me to tell our family stories.

Appreciation is expressed to three individuals who have been my mentors and who took the time to read the manuscript of the first edition and provide helpful suggestions for its improvement. These three friends and colleagues are Bill Rogers, Milton Snyder, and Richard Underwood.

I would like to thank the people and churches who have walked with me and my family during our crises. They have truly become family for us when crisis came home.

CONTENTS

PREFACE

This book begins with the assumption that all families, Christian and non-Christian, face crises. Faith in God may give strength to cope, but faith doesn't provide immunity to crisis.

When I think of crisis, I think of a time of extreme difficulty and anxiety. When families face a crisis, the intensity of the situation causes the family to focus its energy on the crisis. Sometimes the crisis causes them immediately to drop what they are doing and tend to the crisis or the person in crisis. Some crises may be more developmental in nature and somewhat less acute. In any case, when crisis comes home, the family routine is interrupted as the crisis takes center stage.

The purpose of this book is to help you and your family prepare for, deal with, and learn from crises in your home. Perhaps this book will also help you help others in crisis. The Bible is full of examples of how God's people, with homes grounded in the faith, faced crisis after crisis. These biblical personalities and families were not hopeless because of the crisis. Instead, their faith in God buoyed them, giving them hope for the future and strength to cope in the present.

Hope is possible, even in what might seem like a hopeless situation. It is the purpose of this book to point beyond the crisis, beyond the hopelessness, to the Bible and the biblical message of hope. If this book helps you and your family draw on the inner resources of your faith in God, if it better enables you to give and receive care from your church family, and if it helps you discover ways to draw strength from other family members, then the purpose has been accomplished.

I will be sharing experiences of how crisis has come home to my family and me. Others have also given permission to relate their crises, and for this I am grateful. Prior to and during the writing of this book, I corresponded with and talked to numerous people who described how crisis came home to their families. I am blessed by their stories and testimonies of how their faith brought strength for living. I trust you will be too.

—*John Lepper*

PREFACE TO THE REVISED EDITION

A number of years have passed since I wrote the first edition of this book. The first edition included a portrait of our family; our two girls were then preteens. They are now grown with their own families, children, and careers. They have taught me much as we have moved together through several developmental phases of family life. Allison, who has subsequently majored in journalism, has reviewed this book and made several helpful suggestions.

In these intervening years, my own career has shifted from the leader of family ministry for a state convention to coordinator of the Kentucky Baptist Fellowship, a state affiliate of the Cooperative Baptist Fellowship. I have also continued to maintain a part-time pastoral counseling practice. Both roles have allowed me to assist families and church families in crisis. Regarding church families, of special interest and focus to me has been helping churches during an interim between ministers. Such an event is a crisis of sorts in the life of a church. Heightened anxiety is always present in a congregation during an interim. What I say about families in this book can be applied to church families experiencing a crisis.

My continued work with individuals and couples in a formal counseling setting has taught me much regarding family dynamics. While the basic substance of this book remains true to its original edition, I have been able to include some recent examples of how contemporary families are facing the challenges of a crisis.

Dr. Andrew Lester's book, *Hope in Pastoral Care and Counseling*, has greatly informed my thinking and practice of ministry in recent years. The book helps pastoral counselors refocus the attention of someone in crisis so they can focus on the future and hope. The book is about story, particularly future story.

Every person and family has three stories. The first relates to our past. The second relates to our current situation. The third relates to our future. The story of one's past may be painful, and indeed it lingers into the present. Family systems theorists use words like transgenerational emotional force or transgenerational residue to describe issues families currently face that have carried over from past generations.

Remembering stories of our past can trigger anger and pain. Our current issues can cause a narrow focus on our present pain or problems. While the past may haunt us and the present may consume us, our real energy lies in our future story. All of us tend to live toward our future story, whether that story is negative or positive, hopeful or despairing. Andy Lester reminds us that the real energy for change comes in reshaping one's future story.

Hope, says Lester, has much to do with one's future story. Families in crisis may need time to process the pain of the past and present. But if families are to move forward, at some point they need to begin reconstructing their future story. Only then can they begin the journey from despair to hope.

John Lepper
Louisville, Kentucky
April 2009

Chapter 1

CRISIS COMES HOME TO CHRISTIANS

He makes his sun rise on the evil and on the good, and sends rain on the righteous and on the unrighteous. (Matthew 5:45b, NRSV)

The call came at 5:00 in the morning. We were awakened from sleep to learn that my father had died. The call was not only an interruption of sleep; it was an interruption of our Christmas plans. But death never comes at the "right" time. Just three days before Christmas, and more than 700 miles from my hometown, our family would improvise the holiday plans this year.

Just as pain in one part of our physical body affects the whole body, pain in one family member affects the whole family. The impact of my father's death may have been most intense for me. However, it also affected my wife and our two daughters, ages nine and twelve. This crisis of grief became the focus of our family's thinking, feeling, and activities for days and weeks to come.

The Christmas tree that sat in our dining room remained undecorated. Presents were hastily opened. We made adjustments in order to have some semblance of a family Christmas celebration but also take care of our "grief work." There was a strange mix of emotions and experiences.

The two major grief experiences in my life occurred first when I was a teenager and now during adulthood. When I was fifteen years of age, my mother was hospitalized for exploratory surgery. Three days later she died. Crisis came home to my family and me on both occasions.

Each of these two grief experiences was shaped by, among other things, my particular stage of the life cycle at the time. At fifteen I was dealing with two adolescent issues: (1) my role in life and (2) reality and responsibility. With the sudden death of Mother, I lost the primary person in my life who provided me emotional support. As a middle-aged adult, now coping with Dad's death, I was torn between my need to express my personal grief and my desire to "take care" of those around me during their grief.

While the death of Mother during my adolescence brought about a vacuum of nurture, the loss of Dad during my middle adult years brought about a vacuum of wisdom and strength to face responsibilities. Even though I had lived independently from Dad for more than two decades, I knew he was always there if I needed him. I loved and respected Dad for the strength of his Christian character, his devotion to family, and his love for God. It had not dawned on me until his death, but he was for me what one person described as a barrier or buffer between the adult child and the world. I experienced mortality shock as Dad's death removed the buffer between me and death. I'm now the oldest surviving generation, and I feel strangely and mysteriously more vulnerable to death.

This death brought about a crisis not just for me, but for our whole family. We longed for a normal family Christmas; we longed for a normal family life again. No amount of wishing would bring this about because we were squarely in the middle of an unavoidable family crisis. As a matter of fact, we were experiencing one of the more ordinary forms of crisis. Even though every family's bereavement is unique, death is a crisis all families experience at one time or another.

WHEN CRISIS COMES HOME

Pause to consider the title of this book. The beginning word of the title, "when," points to our first assumption. "When" suggests that crisis *will* come home to families. Saying "*if* crisis comes home" misrepresents the facts. Crisis is not always present. Rather, as the title suggests, crisis will sooner or later come home to every family.

Our title could be a question: "Why does crisis come home?" Even though this question is not raised in the title, it is probably raised in your mind. People often say we should not question why. In real life, however, I hear people asking that question—even if it is asked in a roundabout way. Nowhere do I find an admonition in the Bible to refrain from asking why. In fact, we hear this question on the lips of numerous Bible personalities. Job, Moses, and Paul are three of many examples. We will address this question more fully as we look at the deeper issues of suffering, hope, and the providence of God.

The second word of the title, "crisis," describes what the book is all about. We will look at four categories of crises families face. First, let's arrive at a suitable definition for the word. We can gain our first clue from the Chinese symbol for the word "crisis." This Chinese symbol is made up of two parts. One part means danger; the second means opportunity. Crisis brings both an opportunity for growth as well as a danger to our well-being.

Our second clue comes from the Latin and Greek words from which we get our word "crisis." The Greek word means decision; the Latin means to decide. A crisis, then, is a decisive point; a fork in the road. A decision must be made as to the direction of travel.

A crisis is an event or series of events that, when taken together, form a difficult or even harmful situation for a person or family. However, a crisis is more than a difficult situation. A crisis occurs because we perceive the difficult situation as harmful or stressful. A crisis is present when the difficult situation seems overwhelming to those involved.

The last word in our title is "home," which points to the fact that this book is primarily about family crisis and not personal crisis. Though we cannot avoid the latter, our focus is on crises faced within the home or family. The use of the word "home" also points to another presupposition upon which this book is based, namely, it is impossible to have a crisis only as an individual.

We are inextricably interconnected. What affects one family member ultimately, and often quickly, affects all family members. This truth became clear recently when as I sat with a married couple months after the wife discovered that her husband was having an affair. His indiscretion came to light after about three months of regular "secret" meetings with a close friend of the family, a young lady she described as "one of my closest friends." The family was immediately thrown into panic. He quit his job as a worship pastor; they separated for a time and entered into counseling with a Christian counselor. During these days, the marriage could be characterized as being on life support. In a few weeks they decided to move from a midwestern city back to their hometown. It was then that they entered into counseling with me. I've seen the couple for more than a year, and the whole family continues to feel the effects of this crisis.

Some months after the couple entered counseling, they revealed that their preadolescent children were having difficulty adjusting. It was then that I referred them to a counselor specializing in children, who met with them while Mom sat on the sidelines. The children played with toys and drew on a white board. During these sessions, Mom became aware of the depth of hurt and sadness her children felt as a result of their family crisis.

Again, it is *impossible* to have a crisis alone. Like a stone thrown into a placid lake, a crisis causes ripples that span into many lives. Personal crisis has ripples that reach the immediate family and even extended family members. For this reason, this book looks at family crisis and not only individual crisis.

But to say we are talking about family only compounds our focus. Our society's understanding of family has changed. What used to be the traditional family has evolved in recent years in America. If you think of family as only homes with two parents and two children in which the father works outside the home and the mother serves as homemaker, you cover only a small segment of our population.

When the word "home" is used in this book, it refers to the variety of ways family is experienced. If you are a single parent with two children at home, this book is for you. If you are part of a traditional home where the father/husband is the provider and the mother/wife is homemaker, this book is for you. If you are part of a blended family where one or more children are present from a previous marriage, this book is for you. If you are retired and living with or without a spouse, this book is for you.

A single person reminded me recently that even though she is not married, she considers her best friend with whom she lives to be family. Traditional definitions of family are changing. However, no matter how much our families differ, we all face a crisis sooner or later.

WAYS CHRISTIAN FAMILIES FACE CRISIS TODAY

Let's look at four categories of ways in which Christian families experience crisis. These are not meant as rigid classifications but instead as a way of thinking about the scope and variety of crises Christian families face.

(1) Acute Crises. These might include grief over the loss of a loved one or anticipatory grief because of the terminal illness of a family member; hospitalization of a family member; the adjustment a family must make following a job change and move; financial disruption following a job loss or layoff. Some acute crises are uncommon or bizarre. These might include freak accidents or out-of-the-ordinary events like the killing of children on a playground.

(2) Social Crises. These include divorce, alcohol and drug abuse, physical and emotional abuse, AIDS, and the adjustments stepfamilies must make.

(3) Developmental Crises. These relate to events like marriage, childbearing, the childhood and adolescent years of a family member, the middle adult years, the empty-nest years, retirement, and aging.

(4) Disaster-related Crises. These are brought about by a tornado, flood, hurricane or other community-wide disaster or traumatic accident. Another example is war, or the threat of war, particularly when family members are involved in the fighting.

These categories and descriptions do not exhaust the ways crisis comes home to Christian families. Rather, the list is intended to be suggestive of the kinds of crises families face. We will look more closely at the ways each type of crisis comes about, providing examples of each. Before we do, stop and think about your family and the crisis or crises you may have experienced.

Personal Learning Activity

As you think about the crises your family has faced, consider the family in which you grew up. Do you recall a crisis related to one of the above categories? Jot down the nature of the crisis and list its category.

_____

_____

_____

_____

_____

ACUTE CRISES

In your church, and maybe even in your family, an acute crisis may be coming home right now. A crisis is acute when it comes about suddenly and brings sharp distress. Though it may happen directly to only one family member, the entire family feels the impact and focuses on the situation. Even small children are intuitively aware of family distress. Though the situations might begin as developmental or disaster-related crises, any category of crisis has the potential of becoming acute. When we speak of an acute crisis, we mean the more ordinary kinds of sudden trauma families experience.

Grief

The loss of a family member or significant friend brings grief. Though each family member's grief is unique, response to a loss typically flows through a normative process. Those who work with grieving persons tell us it is normal for the grief process to last from eighteen months to two years, sometimes longer.

The initial reaction to learning of the death of a loved one is often shock. This is particularly true upon hearing the news of an unexpected death. Following the initial shock, numbness sets in. This is the body's way of absorbing the shock. When the numbness wears off, the grieving person may begin to experience a flood of emotions. This is often manifested through crying. During the grief process, the bereaved person struggles with reality. What one's mind knows to be a fact, his or her emotions want to reject as fantasy. It is difficult to let go.

Guilt and anger are often experienced simultaneously. The grieving person may experience intense guilt as he thinks about what might have been done to save the person's life. Guilt is also stirred by remembering unkind words or actions directed toward the deceased during her life. A person may feel angry with the doctor for not doing more, with the deceased person for dying, or even with God. A vicious circle can result as anger triggers feelings of guilt for being angry.

Loneliness and feelings of depression are typical experiences in the months following the death. As we encounter the usual places or things that remind us of the dead person, our flood of emotions may return. After my father's death, this periodic flood of emotions was often triggered during a worship service when one of my father's favorite hymns was sung.

People say time helps heal the hurt of grief. This means grief is a process; it's not something we overcome instantly. However, just because a certain amount of time has lapsed doesn't mean the hurt of grief is healed. When a significant loss occurs, the person experiencing the loss needs time to work through the mix of emotions.

Grief is work. When one deals with rather than dismisses the loss, he or she begins the process of accepting the loss. The bereaved can begin to see light. The light of hope gradually overtakes dark days of depression.

The stages of grief are not always as clear as the above description might suggest. Each person's grief is unique. Nevertheless, it is a process, and it is normal to experience a variety of emotions. The fact that you are a Christian does not provide immunity to grief, nor does it allow you to bypass the normal emotions related to grief. Being a Christian does offer hope for the future as well as strength to cope in the present.

Anticipatory Grief

Another form of acute crisis is anticipatory grief. Our family experienced this kind of difficulty for several months. After my father's funeral, we drove from Florida to North Carolina to visit my wife's mother.

The joys of Christmas were overshadowed by our grief related to my father's death and also by our anxiety that this might be our last Christmas with Mrs. Jackson. The cancer discovered several years ago now brought about a rapid decline in her health.

In addition to celebrating Christmas by exchanging gifts, we found occasion to remember the good times by looking at family albums. Childhood poses of my wife, her brother, and her two sisters brought laughter. It was a lighthearted time as the family told stories about events related to the pictures.

The conversation grew more serious as Mrs. Jackson took the opportunity to talk about her death and her legal will. She knew her life was coming to its end, and she addressed her own anticipatory grief by setting her house in order. Our family conversation that evening was therapeutic, but it heightened our awareness of her decline and also marked the beginning of prolonged distress for our family.

In the months that followed, roles were reversed for Connie as the child became the parent. She made several trips home to care for her mother. She also became the focus of strength and decision-making for her mother. Even though her mother was miles away, almost every waking moment found our family focused on this situation.

Our family experienced the typical emotional stages related to anticipatory grief. Upon learning of Mrs. Jackson's cancer, we experienced shock and numbness. Though some people pass through a flood of emotions characterized by panic, we experienced more denial and disbelief. The conversations at Christmas helped us deal with the reality of Mrs. Jackson's impending death. As the reality of her imminent death dawned on us, we experienced anger. "Why could this be happening to us? Why was something so bad happening to such a good person?" We sometimes misdirected our anger at one another. Sometimes people pull back emotionally and/or physically from the dying person to avoid pain.

Though I cannot give an example in our family's experience, a typical response during anticipatory grief is that of bargaining. A person may try to bargain with God, promising, for example, to be a better Christian if God will bring healing.

Our family experienced periods of depression, despair, and sometimes guilt. Though it was never said in so many words, our guilt was mysteriously connected to our anger. It is normal to feel angry with the terminally-ill patient, but the feeling that quickly follows is one of guilt for feeling anger at such a vulnerable person. I felt guilt for unkind or sharp words I had said. I regretted not getting to know and appreciate Mrs. Jackson much earlier. I felt guilty for not working harder to develop a more intimate relationship with such a strong, yet quiet, Christian. I was angry with myself for this failure.

Anticipatory grief, like bereavement after a loss, is a process individual to each person.

Hospitalization

Another ordinary crisis faced by Christian families is that of hospitalization. One family member's hospitalization disrupts the family routine. Parents experience the pain of their children vicariously. When children are hospitalized, school is missed and parents may go without sleep and miss work. This is complicated by the fact that both spouses may work outside the home.

Hospitalization in a single-parent home can add to an already stressed situation. A person has only so much energy, and a single parent is further stretched by the hospitalization of a family member. When other small children are in the home, childcare is necessary. When a parent is hospitalized, the child may feel deprived of care or even abandoned.

Mental or Emotional Disorders

The psychiatric hospitalization of a family member brings a unique crisis. Though mental illness and emotional disorders do not carry the stigma they once did, the family member with a psychological problem is often misunderstood. After all, mental problems may not be as visible as physical problems. The diagnosis and treatment of mental conditions are frequently confusing to the untrained. Add to this the belief or suspicion that mental problems are self-inflicted, and you begin to understand the unique impact of a psychiatric hospitalization.

Moving

Another form of acute crisis occurs when a family member changes jobs and the family is required to move. Giving up familiar places and usual faces, leaving friends for a new geographical location, is an uprooting. The adjustment that occurs is a form of grief. Adults and children alike find it difficult to say "good-bye" to the old and "hello" to the new.

Uncommon or Bizarre Kinds of Acute Crises

Family crises in this category are rare but do occur, even to Christian families. A missionary family in Ecuador was struck by an uncommon crisis. James Parrish, a church planter from Texas, and two of his sons stopped at a gasoline station for fuel. The father was standing at the back of the truck when the cab suddenly burst into flames. He was able to pull his seven-year-old son, Stephen, from the fire but could not reach the three-year-old, John. Mr. Parrish and his older son were burned severely; the younger son died in the fire. At the time of this bizarre accident, Mrs. Parrish was at home with their other son, Micah, age five.[1]

On a normal September workday at a printing plant in Louisville, Kentucky, a gunman walked past a guard and opened fire with an AK-47 assault weapon. He combed three floors for thirty minutes. In a rage, he fired at random, then turned a pistol on himself. Seven people lay dead and thirteen were severely wounded.[2]

These incredible and horrifying events cause trauma for the victims and their families. Such incidents seem so foreign to the norm of life that our senses want to reject them as fantasy. But they are real indeed for those caught in the crossfire. Families in such situations desperately need a word of hope and concern from Christian friends.

Often the suddenness and uncommonness of this misfortune adds to the difficulty of facing the crisis. As with any kind of crisis that occurs without warning, it can be difficult to accept the reality of what has happened. Because of the complexity of such a crisis, working through the grief process is sometimes delayed because of more immediate concerns. For example, the Parrishes, the missionary family in Ecuador, said they had to delay their grief for the son who died because of their more immediate concerns of caring for the son who lived.

SOCIAL CRISES

In unprecedented numbers, crises related to social trends are coming home to Americans. *Newsweek* magazine reported in 1990 that the divorce rate had doubled since 1965, and projections indicated that six out of ten marriages would end in divorce.[3] The actual divorce rate has fluctuated in recent years, with some sources revising this downward to roughly 43 percent. But as recently as 2002, the Census Bureau placed the number near 50 percent.[4]

The percentage of households headed by a single parent almost doubled from 1970—when it stood at 5 percent—to 9 percent in 1994. However, this percentage showed little variation from 1994 through 2006. In 2006, the Census Bureau also reported that just over two-thirds (67 percent) of children lived with married parents. This means that almost one in three children live in other household configurations, such as with grandparents, with a single parent, or with unmarried parents.[5]

Examples of the pain and suffering in our homes abound. By the mid-1980s, child abuse reached epidemic proportions, with an average of 456,000 cases of abuse reported annually.[6] A more recent statistic appears on the website Childhelp.org. This organization reports that an estimated 906,000 children are victims of abuse and neglect every year.

Childhelp.org lists these consequences of child abuse:

- 80 percent of young adults who had been abused have some kind of psychiatric disorder by age 21.
- Abused children are 25 percent more likely to experience teen pregnancy.
- Children who experience child abuse and neglect are 59 percent more likely to be arrested as a juvenile and 28 percent more likely to be arrested as an adult.
- Almost 15 percent of all men in prison in the USA were abused as children and over one-third of all women in prison were abused as children.
- Children who have been sexually abused are two and a half times more likely to develop alcohol abuse.
- Children who have been sexually abused are almost four times more likely to develop drug addictions.
- Nearly two-thirds of the people in treatment for drug abuse reported being abused as children.[7]

Another study pointed out that in 1990, child abuse occurred in up to an estimated 60 percent of families in the United States.[8]

Divorce
The subject of divorce has been a difficult topic for Christians to discuss. We have the weighty task of upholding the biblical ideal for families while also reaching out to share God's grace. Divorce is not reserved for people outside the church. What church, indeed what family, has not been touched by divorce? The emotional response to divorce is similar to that of grief over death. Divorce marks the death of a marriage relationship; it marks a loss, and loss is experienced like grief. In many cases, especially when children are involved, the relationship continues even if the marriage ends.

Stepfamilies
A trend related to divorce is the increase of stepfamilies. Two-thirds of divorced and widowed individuals remarry. Only about 50 percent of children in the United States spend their entire childhoods living with both natural parents. More than 1,000 stepfamilies are formed daily in the United States with about 500,000 adults becoming new stepparents annually.[9] One-third of all children entering stepfamilies were born to an unmarried mother rather than having divorced parents.[10]

Being part of a stepfamily may not seem like crisis until you consider that every member of a stepfamily has experienced a significant loss. While the loss may be unrelated to death, it is just as real and maybe even more traumatic. Unless the grief and loss are appropriately addressed, each stepfamily member brings unresolved grief to the new relationship, adding to the stress of being part of a new family.

Stepfamilies have the challenge of learning new roles and ways of relating. They must learn to blend values, histories, traditions, expectations, and divided loyalties. What may seem like a simple matter (scheduling visits, for example) can become complicated and almost unmanageable at times.

Alcohol and Drug Abuse

According to the Gallup organization, alcohol and drug abuse is the most serious social problem in our society. Alcohol abuse affects not only those who drink but those related to the consumer. Forty-one percent of Americans say they have suffered in one way or another because of someone else's drinking. The *Journal of the American Medical Association* reports that alcohol contributes to 100,000 deaths annually.[11]

While these statistics are alarming, the good news is that there has been a decrease in the number of drinking alcoholics (as opposed to recovering alcoholics) in recent years (from 5.5 million to 4.5 million).[12] Also, because of new laws and changing attitudes about drinking, highway fatalities have been on a downward trend.

In spite of these positive trends, family crisis related to alcohol abuse continues to be a major problem. Even more alarming is the long-term effect of alcoholism on family members. An array of recent publications and organizations has emerged, speaking to lifelong struggles of the adult child of an alcoholic family.[13]

Physical and Emotional Abuse

In recent years, an area receiving much attention is that of abusive behavior. Whether this problem has grown or whether media attention and reporting methods only make it appear greater is debatable. The fact is, however, that abusive behavior is present to an alarming degree in our society. Physical and emotional abuse can place families in a continuous state of crisis.

A Christian woman reported to her pastoral counselor a pattern of abusive behavior by her husband. He regularly stayed out drinking all hours of the night. When he arrived home, he often awakened her with abusive language and behavior. Because of the fact that she never knew when he would come home, she had difficulty sleeping, sometimes spontaneously waking while her whole body shook.

Abuse runs the gamut from incestuous relationships to date abuse, from battery on a spouse to child abuse. Victimized family members often cover for their abusers, which only compounds the problem. Such family secrets cause dysfunctional families to appear healthy to those on the outside. But the lives of those who are part of such a family are filled with physical and emotional pain. Scars from abuse cut deep and can last a lifetime. If your past or present has been tainted with abuse, you know the pain all too well. You also know the lifelong struggle this brings to relationships and the difficulty in experiencing healing. Problems like these require professional help, but the shame families experience often causes them to resist seeking such assistance.

AIDS

The word "AIDS" causes us to shudder. A word introduced into our vocabulary just a few decades ago, it now refers to a disease that threatens every community. An exact count is not possible, but in 2006 there were estimates that about a million people in the U.S. were infected with HIV, the virus that causes AIDS. While future projections of AIDS abound, no one knows for sure how many people will become infected. Better treatment has improved the quality of life and longevity of persons with HIV and AIDS, but this continues to be a worldwide issue of major concern to families.

Christians are not immune to AIDS. Kip and Millie McConnell ministered in Alaska for more than thirty years. Kip found it necessary to undergo heart bypass surgery. Because of the loss of blood, he needed a transfusion. In the early days of AIDS, the blood supply was not monitored, and Kip received AIDS-infected blood. Kip was a man of God who had given his entire life in service to others in the name of Jesus Christ. His last two years of life brought excruciating pain and caused his family and friends almost unbearable heartache.

A minister friend with whom I've worked had a son who suffered from AIDS. As is often the case, the family stood by helplessly and watched as his body became emaciated. Toward the end of his life, the son became blind and sores covered his flesh. This family took a chance and revealed their situation to their church family. They (both parents and the son with AIDS) attended several Sunday school classes to tell their story. Even though the words did not come easy, their openness helped them deal with their pain. The church family grew significantly as well.

DISASTER-RELATED CRISES

As I revise this book, our nation faces an economic crisis. The economic crisis of 2008 and following has touched virtually everyone in America and countless others around the world. Businesses have failed even as millions of people have lost their jobs. Some of us baby boomers who were nearing retirement watched as the crisis decimated our investments. At this writing, the situation looks bleak. The worldwide economic crisis is a social disaster affecting a large number of people.

When I wrote this section in the first edition of this book, many families in our community were experiencing disaster. Tornadoes ripped through several states, destroying whole towns. Homes were swept away and century-old trees became debris as the tornados unleashed their fury.

I heard the tornado warnings around midnight. After waking my wife and children, we made immediate arrangements to spend the night in our basement. Our experience was only a slight annoyance. For some families, it was a genuine crisis as they lost their homes and most of their belongings. Several people were injured even though they took cover in their basements or central rooms. They listened in panic as their homes were blown away over their heads or from around them. One family discovered that a family member, eight-year-old Ross, did not make it to the bathroom where they all crouched as the tornado blew away their house. After the storm, they discovered Ross standing at the edge of the yard, only slightly hurt and a bit baffled. He had been picked up by the winds and deposited 150 feet from where the house had stood.[14]

We may not think much about the traumatic crisis a natural or social disaster can bring to families. After all, unless it happens in our neighborhood or to our family, the news reports can seem remote.

Hurricanes and earthquakes are other examples of natural disasters. Recent years have brought this to mind much more clearly. Just the words "Hurricane Katrina," evoke dramatic images of the devastation of the Gulf Coast and New Orleans. At first it seemed that New Orleans had narrowly escaped the brunt of the storm, but then two levees broke. New Orleans became submerged, and thousands of people fled their homes for higher ground. Ten thousand people huddled in grim circumstances in the Superdome. Ninety thousand square miles in the Gulf Coast were affected by this disaster. About three million people were without electricity. During the two weeks after the hurricane, as many as a million people were evacuated to other areas, most to neighboring states but some as far away as Rhode

Island. Hundreds of communities were touched by this disaster as they received people fleeing from the storm and floodwaters.

There was also the Indian Ocean tsunami of 2004. On December 26, 2004, great earthquakes deep in the earth shook the ground violently, unleashing a series of waves that sped across the Indian Ocean at the speed of a jet plane. By day's end, more than 150,000 people across 11 countries were dead or missing, and millions more were homeless.

Another disaster, though not natural, can be caused by a violent accident. Plane crashes, bus wrecks, and passenger train derailments affect scores of people and sometimes traumatize whole communities.

On a beautiful Sunday morning some years ago, I traveled Interstate 71, passing Carrolton, Kentucky, on my way to a speaking engagement. Using the travel time to meditate, I didn't turn on the radio that morning. Later I realized I passed the site of one of the worst bus crashes in history. The accident had occurred only a few hours before, and the debris was barely cleared away by the time I passed the scene.

A drunken driver, traveling north in a southbound lane, collided with a bus full of teenagers and chaperones who were returning from a church outing at a theme park near Cincinnati, Ohio. Twenty-four people died in the fiery blaze as the survivors looked on in horror. Those who were able to get to safety will carry physical or emotional scars for the rest of their lives.[15]

War or the threat of war is also a social disaster since it touches whole communities and nations. The events of September 11, 2001, are engraved in the memories of those of who witnessed the events on that day. Who among us will ever forget the sight of the collapsing World Trade Center towers, the smoldering field in Pennsylvania, or the gaping wound left in the Pentagon? The nation was disrupted that day and for weeks and months following; families touched by death on that day still search for healing.

Wars in Iraq and Afghanistan have brought about the deployment of hundreds of thousands of military and civilian personnel. The lives of individuals, families, and institutions around the world are still disrupted. Many local hospitals, police departments, fire departments, and even churches are short-handed as a result of the call-up. Families (and indeed institutions and whole communities) are forced to cope with the absence of loved ones and the uncertainty of their return. Those who do return come back with deep emotional pain, along with the possibility of lasting physical pain.

In these and other disasters, entire communities face crisis. Christian families finds themselves in the unique position of dealing with their own trauma while also reaching out to assist others who find themselves in the same situation.

Wayne Oates, one of the founders of the pastoral care and counseling movement, has suggested that communities typically move through seven phases during the course of a disaster. These include (1) warning, (2) threat, (3) impact, (4) inventory, (5) rescue, (6) remedy, and (7) recovery.[16]

Communication is important during the early warning stages of a crisis. Lack of information or misinformation fuels rumors and intensifies the stress of a social disaster. During the second phase, that of threat, the need is to help families remain calm, avoid panic, and take necessary precautions. The disaster occurs during the impact phase. Following this, families begin to take inventory of their personal and physical losses. The rescue phase brings out the best and worst in people. Assistance needs to match the need without exhibition, unnecessary risk-taking, and exaggerated activity. The remedy and recovery phases follow the disaster as families try to put their lives back together. Physical restoration following a disaster may take a year or more. Emotional recovery could take as long and should be just as intentional.

The federal government, the Red Cross, churches, and other agencies offer assistance to families displaced by social disaster. But all the agencies in the world cannot remove the fact that these families must deal with loss and face the task of rebuilding their lives.

My friend Charlie Gatton has been house leader for the construction of more than fifty Habitat for Humanity homes. The amazing thing is that Charlie began his volunteer work with Habitat at age seventy-four—about ten years ago. Charlie has also been house leader for "Extreme Build," a project in southeastern Kentucky where volunteers build a house in a week and a half. Charlie is an engineer and received much experience in his career with the railroad. In that capacity, he was responsible for maintaining the railroad tracks, including rebuilding tracks when disasters destroyed them.

He tells of the time Hurricane Camille hit the Gulf Coast in August 1969. Realizing the storm was on its way and recognizing the severity of the storm (it was actually rated as more intense than Katrina), Charlie and others with the railroad hired self-contained crews to head toward the Gulf Coast and await the call for specific instructions. One crew waited out the storm in Birmingham and then proceeded to the coast. The day following the storm, Charlie and others with the railroad surveyed the damage from a low-flying airplane. They discovered that 22 miles of tracks were destroyed, much of them upended, turned upside down, and moved some distance from the original roadbed. With a great deal of coordinated effort of railroad personnel and four self-contained crews, the tracks were rebuilt and trains were traveling them within twenty-one days.

This story illustrates what can be accomplished in a short period of time with skilled and coordinated effort. But while property may be restored in a matter of days, the results of disasters on human lives and families can take much longer to resolve.

DEVELOPMENTAL CRISES

A developmental crisis may not be as painful or focused as other kinds of crises; however, this crisis lasts longer and may be felt differently since it is often dissipated over a longer period of time. Also, since the developmental crisis comes about more slowly, we may grow accustomed to it and not recognize it as a crisis. Developmental crises, though painful, are a normal part of family life, even for Christians and Christian families.

Let's walk together through some developmental crises of a typical family. On any given Saturday in June, and in any given church, a young couple joins hands in the holy estate of matrimony. They face developmental crisis number one as they adjust to each other. In his book, *Christ and the Seasons of Marriage*, John Killinger says newlyweds have four tasks as they begin their life together: discovery, negotiation, renunciation, and love.[17]

How many people have you heard say, "We just thought we knew each other before we married"? The fact is, certain dimensions of us become apparent only in the marriage relationship. As differences come to light, the art of negotiation becomes important. If this hurdle is surpassed, both husband and wife are called to practice the art of renunciation. As the couple learns to give and take, love becomes more than an adolescent stirring. Love for one another has the potential of growing to fit the description in 1 Corinthians 13.

Throughout their lives, this couple will face numerous crisis points. A child is born and becomes the focus of the couple's energy. More children may be born; with each, a new challenge arises.

As the children attend their first day in school, they must adjust to an outside world while parents face the challenge of gradually letting go. In what seems like a short season, the childhood years pass and puberty arrives. With puberty comes adolescence. During this phase of our family's life, I said to people only half jokingly, "Our whole family is currently going through adolescence!" When one family member is a teenager, the whole family is stressed by this adolescent adjustment. I say that even though that phase of our family life was filled neither with acute crises nor with acting out on the part of our teens.

The teenage years in many families are a turbulent time. Teens seek to claim their freedom, often without accepting commensurate responsibility. Parents struggle to turn loose while longing to hold on. Often, about this same time, adults must care for their aging parents, thus becoming part of what has been called the "sandwich generation." Decisions families face about how best to provide care for an incapacitated family member bring about pain and crisis.

Next comes the time when children grow up and leave home. A child may marry or remain single. If he/she marries, then comes the "crisis" of becoming in-laws and grandparents. At some point, the long-awaited day of retirement comes, bringing with it yet another set of crises. Declining health, physical or mental, of one family member brings a crisis home to the whole family once more.

These few brief paragraphs cannot capture the pain and joy, the ebb and flow, that come with the seasons of life. For with the seasons of life come the developmental crises of life.

CONCLUSION

We can understand family crisis in one of four categories: (1) acute crises, (2) social crises, (3) disaster-related crises, and (4) developmental crises.

Christians have no special power to avoid crisis. We cannot choose the changes and chances that will befall us in life. However, we can choose our responses, and our response to each crisis point prepares us for the next one. If we are overwhelmed by one crisis, the chances of the next crisis becoming even more overwhelming are greater. However, if we can grow through each crisis, then we are better able to withstand the next crisis.

Even though Christians have no special power to avoid crises, we do have a special coping power. Christians have an advantage over non-Christians to the extent that we are able to experience the power of Christ within us. This power doesn't necessarily eliminate the crisis, but it can aid us in choosing healthy responses and coping with our trauma.

Personal Learning Activity

Now that we have given examples of the various ways Christians face crises, think about your family—the one you live with right now. Has your current family experienced a crisis related to any of the four categories? If you are a single person, have you experienced a crisis related to any of the four categories? If so, write it down and list the category or categories in which it belongs. You may list more than one crisis, and each crisis may fall into more than one category.

If you listed more than one crisis, choose the one that was most significant for you. Briefly describe the events leading up to and involved in the crisis. Did the crisis become the focus of your energy and/or your family's energy? If so, how?

NAMING THE CRISIS

Before a doctor can truly begin to treat you, he or she must make a diagnosis. Similarly, if you are to move beyond a crisis, you need to name it. A friend of mine is fond of saying, "If you can't name it, you can't fix it." While you may not be a "crisis physician," you know best the nature of your (or your family's) situation. You know where you hurt. As you name the crisis, you gain power to move beyond it.

Using the categories already discussed, here are several ways to identify a family crisis.

1. Name the crisis for your family as a whole. Is the crisis developmental? Is it an acute crisis, either ordinary or uncommon? Is it related to a natural disaster or traumatic occurrence? Is it related to a social disaster? Is it related to societal trends?

2. Help each family member name the crisis for himself or herself. How would individual family members describe the crisis? How does the crisis affect each family member?

3. Name the crisis in terms of your family's life stage. Looking at your family as a unit, what words would you use to name your current developmental stage?

I will illustrate using the crisis our family experienced related to the terminal cancer and ultimate death of my wife's mother. Let's begin by naming the crisis as a family. Our knowledge of Mrs. Jackson's cancer and declining health caused our family to suffer what could be termed anticipatory grief. Our crisis grew more acute as her condition worsened, and became most acute upon her death. Her situation was the focus of numerous family conversations. While we never used the words "acute crisis," we talked openly about our feelings of grief and loss.

We all experienced grief, but each experienced it in a different way. Connie was losing a mother, her last surviving parent. The intensity of her grief was heightened beyond this fact because of the amount of responsibility she assumed for her mother's care and decision-making. Our children were losing a dear grandmother. They had spent several weeks at her home almost every summer of their lives. "Mama J" had loved them and spent time with them, patiently playing games and helping them learn a variety of skills. The children were the joy of her life, and her granddaughters dearly loved her. As for me, I was experiencing the loss of a friend and person who had become a substitute parent for me. As each of us expressed our own loss, we were better able to face our grief. By not denying or avoiding the imminent death of a parent and grandparent, we were able to face the crisis.

The third step in naming the crisis was in terms of our family's life stage. This became clear as we recognized ourselves as middle-aged adults, a part of the sandwich generation. Connie and I were pulled toward our own family as we faced numerous responsibilities. We were also pulled toward our family of origin as we assisted them in coping with life and death.

Personal Learning Activity
Refer back to the crisis you listed in Personal Learning the previous activity.

1. Name the crisis for your family as a whole.

_____

_____

_____

2. How would individual family members describe the crisis?

_____

_____

_____

3. What words would you use to name your family's developmental stage at the time of the crisis?

_____

_____

SUMMARY

In this chapter we began with the assumption that family crisis is inevitable. We looked at the fact that a crisis presents us with both danger and opportunity. We then considered the scope and variety of crises Christians and Christian families face today. Though these types do not exhaust the ways crisis comes home, we listed (1) acute crises, (2) social crises, (3) developmental crises, and (4) disaster-related crises. In the chapter's closing portion, we explored naming the crisis as the first step toward claiming it as an opportunity.

In the next chapter, we will consider how a crisis causes us to search for meaning in a desperate situation. Our goal will be to find hope in what seems hopeless.

NOTES

1. "Missionaries Say 'God Is In Control,'" *The Christian Index*, 2 August 1990, 5.

2. Rob Cunningham, "Drug Taken by Wesbecker Not Known to Cause Violence," *The (Louisville KY) Courier Journal*, 28 October 1989, metro section, p. 7.

3. Jerrold K. Footlick, "What Happened to the Family?" *Newsweek* (special ed.) (Winter/Spring 1990): 16.

4. "Divorce Rates," Americans for Divorce Reform, http://www.divorcereform.org/rates.html#anchor1223885.

5. U. S. Census Bureau, "Single-Parent Households Showed Little Variation Since 1994, Census Bureau Reports," news release, 27 March 2007.

6. "New Push to Guard Children," *U.S. News and World Report*, 7 May 1984, 20.

7. Childhelp, *National Child Abuse Statistics: Child Abuse in America*, compiled from the National Institute on Drug Abuse 2000 Report and Child Abuse Neglect Study by Arthur Becker-Weidman PhD, http://www.childhelp.org/resources/learning-center/statistics, 2006.

8. Joe E. Richardson, "Child Abuse and the Church," *Search* (Winter 1990): 40.

9. "Family Life/American Style," *Remarriage* 2/8 (August 1985): 32.

10. Stepfamily Foundation, statistics, http://www.stepfamily.org/statistics.html, 2008.

11. J. McGinnis and W. Foege, "Actual Causes of Death in the United States," *Journal of the American Medical Association* 270/18 (10 November 1993): 2208; quoted also in National Council on Alcoholism and Drug Dependence, "Alcoholism and Alcohol-Related Problems: A Sobering Look," July 2000, http://www.ncadd.org/facts/problems.html.

12. Ibid.

13. See, for example, Janet Woititz's *Adult Children of Alcoholics* (1990) and *The Complete ACOA Sourcebook: Adult Children of Alcoholics at Home, at Work and in Love* (2002); Rokelle Lerner, *Daily Affirmations for Adult Children* (1996); Connie Dawson and Jean Illsley Clark, *Growing Up Again: Parenting Ourselves, Parenting Our Children* (2nd ed.,1998), all published by HCI, Deerfield Beach FL.

14. Greg Otolski, "Floyds Knobs Boy Survives Twister Ride," *The (Louisville KY) Courier Journal*, 4 June 1990, news section, p. 1.

15. "Cease Commended for Bus Crash Work," *The Oldham Era*, 2 August 1990, B-8.

16. Wayne E. Oates and Andrew D. Lester, *Pastoral Care in Crucial Human Situations* (Valley Forge PA: Judson Press, 1969) 204.

17. John Killinger, *Christ and the Seasons of Marriage* (Nashville: Broadman Press, 1987) 21.

Chapter 2

MAKING SENSE OF THE SENSELESS

*We know that all things work together for good. . . . Who will separate us from
the love of Christ? Will hardship, or distress, or persecution, or famine, or naked-
ness, or peril, or sword? . . . No, in all these things we are more than conquerors
through him who loved us. (Rom 8:28a, 35, 37, NRSV)*

A family crisis demands the attention of each family member, consuming
time and energy. During more tragic and acute stages of a crisis, we may lose
strength and focus required to accomplish daily responsibilities. We find it
difficult to think about anything else.

Naming the crisis is essential in order to cope and move beyond its
debilitating affects. Even though it is a small beginning, simply categorizing
a crisis is comforting to the mind. We name it in order to gain understanding and move beyond the current situation.

Our minds may grasp for reality while denying what has come to pass.
We may wallow in self-pity, repress feelings, or project false hope onto our
circumstances. We may wonder what might have been done to prevent the
situation, but it's too late for such musing. We are squarely in the middle of
a crisis.

The crisis seems senseless. We are caught between hope and hopelessness. We may have glimpses of light at the end of the tunnel, but much of
the time we see only darkness. The usual answers are trite in the face of our
suffering; these answers may even seem flippant. We want to understand and
exercise our faith, but like the man who approached Jesus after the transfiguration requesting healing for his son, we say, "I believe; help my unbelief!"
(Mark 9:24b, NRSV).

We desire more than anything to regain genuine hope. We need authentic hope to touch us at the depth of our pain. Superficial hope tends to
oversimplify these complex issues. Sometimes biblical verses are imposed on
our suffering and our crises in ways that do not take the gravity of our pain
seriously. Questions raised in the midst of suffering are profound and important. Superficial hope is a puny substitute for the genuine hope found in
Jesus Christ.

When our families face crises, it is sometimes easy to look for a quick fix. More often than not, though, a quick fix adds to our plight. With our desire for the crisis to end, we may repress our suffering and become superficially hopeful. When we do this, we deny the fact that our crisis is causing difficulty. However, to say with our lips that we have hope does not give us hope. When we say we have hope but in reality experience despair, then our hope is superficial.

Another less than helpful response is to repress hope and become cynical. We deny the presence of hope and become skeptical of any hope, real or superficial.

When crisis comes home, our task is to face our questioning squarely as we search for authentic Christian hope. Though it does not come easy, genuine hope is possible, even when we feel crushed by a crisis. Before we think about ways we can claim genuine hope, let's pause a moment for personal reflection.

Personal Learning Activity

1. What superficial words have you heard that failed to offer you genuine hope?

_____

_____

2. What way or ways have you felt like denying hope and becoming cynical or skeptical?

_____

_____

3. What helped you move toward genuine hope?

_____

_____

As often as not, the meaninglessness of suffering crushes us. If we could simply understand the crisis and make sense of our distress, we might move in the direction of wholeness. The act of finding meaning in the crisis helps us begin to rise above our situation and regain hope. As we find meaning, health returns and growth is possible, both for individuals and for families.

Let us face squarely, then, the crisis that has befallen us. We may not choose or cause the crisis, but we can choose the spirit with which we face any situation in life. This choice is an act of the will. Let us make a determination of our wills to avoid the two extremes of denying hope or denying our suffering. Let us walk the middle ground between hopelessness and superficiality, facing our questions and affirming our faith.

We need to consider three broad categories as we seek to make sense of the senseless. The first is the idea of suffering. We must try to arrive at some kind of resolution about its nature and meaning for us. Second, we need a proper understanding and reliance on the providence of God. Third, as we make sense of our suffering and gain an understanding of how God works in the world, we begin to find hope. Let us look at these three areas, realizing that during a crisis they don't always come neatly bundled in individual packages. In the process of making sense of our suffering, we learn to rely on God. As we rely on the providence of God, we often begin to make sense of our suffering and rediscover hope.

MAKING SENSE OF SUFFERING

Let us begin making sense of our crisis by thinking about suffering. We recognize that human suffering is an age-old problem that cannot be fully resolved. Nevertheless, let us struggle together to make sense of this perplexing issue.

I must confess that, at this point, "bumper sticker" theology doesn't work for me. The problem of pain is too big for the answer to be contained in a phrase that can fit on a bumper sticker or church marquee. Neat and tidy rarely seem to offer real help with a crisis.

As I wrote the first edition of this chapter, I noticed the following words on a sign in front of a church: "Don't put a question mark where God puts a period." The implication is that God brings about situations of finality, and therefore we as humans should not question why.

I disagree with that kind of theology. God does not directly cause many things in life, but that's not to say God is absent when we suffer. Human badness and human frailty bring about much suffering for which God can neither be blamed nor credited.

In his classic book *The Problem of Pain*, C. S. Lewis suggests that pain is inherent in our existence as humans. He further suggests that perhaps 80 percent of all human suffering is due to the wickedness of human beings. The fact is, we as humans have the capacity for good and the capacity for evil. We have the capacity to hurt and the capacity to provide healing. Lewis reminds us that humans, not God, have created such things as bombs and bayonets, wars and slavery.[1] The evil or negligence of people brings about much of the crises families encounter. Also, according to Lewis, much suffering cannot be traced to human failings or human sin. Like Job, the crisis we have faced or are facing may not be related to anybody's misdeeds.

How then can we make sense of where God fits regarding suffering? After all, much of the pain in the world, including the pain present in family crises, comes through what have generally been termed "acts of God." Shall we give God the credit for destructive acts that cause untold amounts of pain and suffering? How can we believe that God is both sovereign and good? If God is concerned "for the least of these," why doesn't he do something about a given situation?

These are not new questions. Job had serious questions about God's presence in his predicament. His words may become our words: "Oh, that I knew where I might find him, that I might come even to his dwelling! I would lay my case before him, and fill my mouth with arguments" (Job 23:3-4, RSV).

Thinkers, both religious and otherwise, have grappled with such issues for centuries. Epicurus, a philosopher who lived about 2,500 years ago, raised the question with these words: "If He is both willing and able, which alone is suitable to God, from what source then are evils? Or why does He not remove them?" Epicurus resolved his dilemma by believing that God has no interest in humans.[2] While we may find similar questions on the lips of biblical writers and biblical personalities, their answers are far different than that of the philosopher, the agnostic, or the atheist.

Harry Emerson Fosdick, an American pulpiteer who lived in the first part of the twentieth century, preached a sermon in which he asked the age-old question, "How can we believe in a good God in a world like this?" It is a question you may have asked as you tried to sort out your feelings and thoughts about your family's suffering during a crisis.

Fosdick's answer, though not conclusive, has helped me deal with the pain of crises in my life. We can believe in a good God because God has created a good and law-abiding universe. In this law-abiding universe, Fosdick suggests that all suffering comes from four factors, either by themselves or working together. These four factors are (1) the law-abiding nature of the universe, (2) the progressive nature of human life, (3) the human freedom of choice, (4) and the intermeshed relationships of human life.[3]

Fosdick suggests that all the suffering we experience comes from the "single or conjoint operation of those four factors. Yet if you had omnipotence for an hour, would you eliminate from the universe a single one of them? . . . Everything worthwhile in life also comes from these same four factors whence its tragedies spring."[4] In other words, what gives us the most satisfaction and pleasure in life are the very things, when events go awry, that give us the greatest pain. Let's look at these four factors and observe their significance regarding both pleasure and pain.

Jesus made an observation about the law-abiding nature of the universe when he said God "makes his sun rise on the evil and on the good, and sends rain on the righteous and on the unrighteous" (Matt 5:45b, NRSV). Both evil people and righteous people suffer the consequences of the natural law of gravity if they jump from a tall bridge. Likewise, both receive the blessing of sunshine sent by God. Think of the endless suffering caused by the law-abiding nature of the universe. We may think this law is impersonal, yet the operation of this law is necessary for an orderly and efficient universe.

The second factor, that of the progressive nature of human life, also brings both pleasure and suffering. One area where this factor applies relates to human growth and development. Consider the pain and pleasure experienced by a growing child. How many skinned knees have we received while progressing from crawling to walking to riding a bicycle? This is just a small example of how the principle works in life. Life is a stern teacher as we struggle with the mastery of skills and understanding. While learning is often painful, the failure to learn may be even more painful and disastrous.

God created an unfinished universe and allowed humans the opportunity to participate with God in the improvement of the world. Human growth and development and the progress of mankind do not proceed along a direct path of incline. Rather, we have setbacks and hindrances along the way. These often cause suffering. On the other hand, it is the nature of humanity to gain pleasure and satisfaction from bringing progress to our unfinished world.

The third factor, that of human freedom of choice, also brings both joy and sorrow. God gives humans choices. Often, poor choices bring pain and suffering. Sometimes our choices are ignorant and unwise. Sometimes our choices are blatantly evil. Small and seemingly insignificant choices lead to both little difficulties and major misfortune. In the same manner, choices can lead to great victories and positive advances. The law of seedtime and harvest about which Paul speaks in Galatians applies at this point. Whatever seeds we sow, whether good or bad, will germinate and bear fruit one day.

The fourth factor, the intermeshed relationships of human life, can also bring about great pain and heartache as well as enormous joy. For better or for worse, we are tied together into families, communities, nations, and races. Our evil deeds as well as our acts of charity affect those around us.

God created us in such a fashion that we are intricately bound to one another. Our actions affect not only ourselves but also our families, our communities, and our world. Think of the amount of pleasure we gain from our families. Think also of the amount of pain that is brought about as we see family members suffer or as family members make poor choices.

In our search for meaning in times of crisis, we sometimes look too closely for immediate causes. Fosdick's suggestions help me refocus my attention on broader aspects of God's creation. These broader considerations help me realize that the things that bring me the most joy in life can also bring the greatest pain when combined with poor choices, negligence, or evil.

Instead of placing blame or credit with God for our circumstances, let us remember that God sent his Only Son to bring redemption and salvation to humanity. It may be difficult to reconcile the presence of evil in the world with a good God, but it is far more difficult to explain good in the world without the presence of a good God. While our human understanding about life may lack finality and completeness, we can know personally this good God who gives us the power to surmount the suffering we face as individuals and as families.

This explanation, though incomplete, begins to help us make sense of the senseless. Our need for an explanation of crisis can never be totally fulfilled. The world in which our families live is mysterious. Some events that come our way are inexplicable. Even Jesus never claimed to explain the world. Jesus did claim that he had overcome the world. He promises to share this same overcoming power with his children.

God does not always change the unpleasant situations in our lives. Sometimes God changes *us* for situations. I came to a new understanding of this truth through a series of crises my family and I faced when I was a teenager. When I was fifteen, my mother died unexpectedly. About a year later, while driving to prayer meeting at our church, I had an accident in which a man was killed. The police ruled that the accident was unavoidable, but the man's widow took my dad and me to court. For months it seemed that my world was caving in on top of me. I struggled with guilt and shame related to the accident in spite of the fact that the authorities exonerated me. My pastor preached a sermon using Romans 8:28: "We know that all things work together for good for those who love God, who are called according to his purpose" (NRSV). I came to see that God uses all things that happen to his children for good. That's not to say God causes all things but rather that no matter how bad our situation may be, God is strong enough to use it for our good. It was a message of hope I needed to hear as I tried to make sense of those calamities and as I came to a new understanding of suffering.

Personal Learning Activity

1. What Scripture verse has been meaningful to you as you have tried to make sense of suffering?

_____

_____

2. How have you made sense of crises you or your family have faced?

_____

_____

UNDERSTANDING AND RELYING ON THE PROVIDENCE OF GOD

Perhaps a discussion of God's providence will shed some light, helping us make sense of God's relationship to our suffering. In a general sense, God's providence refers to God's power in creating, ordering, and maintaining the world. Or, to put it another way, God's providence refers to God's goodness as well as God's guiding and sustaining care. Let us consider, then, how God's goodness and power relate to us as humans and specifically how His power relates to our family crises.

The word "providence" comes from two Latin words that mean "to see ahead." The English word "providence" can also mean "to look after."[5] Therefore, to believe in divine providence is to believe that God sees before us and looks after us. Like a person in a tall building overlooking the beginning and ending of a parade, God sees ahead. Once the parade has passed, God continues to look after us with care and concern.

God's work in the lives of the Israelites during their bondage in Egypt is an Old Testament example of how God sees ahead and looks after God's children. The book of Exodus describes how God heard and responded to the cry of the Israelite people as they became slaves to the Egyptians. At the burning bush, Moses came face to face with the great "I AM" of history. God used Moses to free the slaves. God's power was manifested in a series of plagues that brought about their release. Perhaps God's greatest promise to Moses was the promise of God's presence. Moses and the Israelite people were guided by God's caring hand as they departed Egypt and made their way to the promised land.

The last chapter of Deuteronomy describes how Moses went to a mountain and looked over into the promised land (Deut 34:1). Moses was not allowed actually to enter this land, but he saw with his own eyes the land that was promised. Perhaps in this way he experienced the hope found in God's providential care.

As I write this, we are in the season of Lent. This past Sunday was the first Sunday of Lent, and I had occasion to worship at First Baptist Church of Middlesboro, Kentucky. This church follows the liturgical calendar and the minister's sermon related to wilderness and hope.

Pastor Matt DuVall told of an experience that occurred a few years ago during an Ash Wednesday service. Not having grown up in a church that celebrated Ash Wednesday and Lent, this was a new experience for him. The senior pastor coached him, and the two ministers shared leadership related to the imposition of ashes. The congregation came down two aisles for this ritual. The ministers had discussed the need to move toward anyone in the congregation who was unable to walk down front.

As people came forward, Matt imposed ashes in the shape of a cross and spoke the words, "Remember that you are dust, and to dust you shall return," for each worshiper. Toward the close of the service, he noticed that an elderly woman, about ninety years of age, was still sitting toward the back. He started moving toward her and then noticed her getting up. Being sensitive to her, he decided to wait and allow her to walk toward him. She slowly made her way to him even as her age showed in her hunched posture and slow gait. When she arrived in front of him, he stooped down to get on her level and imposed the ashes. As his thumb touched her forehead, he repeated the words, "From dust you were born, and to dust you shall return." Pastor DuVall says, "Her eyes looked straight into mine. I finished and we held our gaze, and then she gave me a wink. It was as if she said, 'Young man, I know what this mortality is all about. I feel it in my bones every day. I feel it in the hours that it takes me to get ready for the day. I know it in the missed sights and lost sounds, in my weak appetite, and the names and faces that seem distantly familiar. It is in the pain in my back and hips and in my failing strength. I see it every day in the empty chairs around the table and the friends that are but a memory.'"

I wonder also if the wink wasn't a way of expressing hope. Perhaps the wink was her way of saying, "I've lived a long time. I know that I came from dust and I'll return to dust. But that's not the whole story. God has been with me through my ninety years of this life, and God will be with me at the end of life and beyond." Like Moses, this person's age and experience allowed her to view the promised land from the mountain. Through the words and experience of the imposition of ashes, her wink conveyed her hope.

It is certainly true that the same God who delivered those people centuries ago from their servitude is still the great "I AM" of history. The promise of God's presence remains true for us today. Our families can count on the providence of God to guide us and care for us in times of crisis. Just as God delivered the Israelite people from captivity, God continues to have the power to deliver us from the pain of family crisis.

The Bible is full of examples of God's providential care. In the Sermon on the Mount, Jesus called his disciples to trust in God's care. Matthew 6:25 records how Jesus urged his hearers not to be anxious for life: "Therefore I tell you, do not worry about your life, what you will eat or what you will drink, or about your body, what you will wear. Is not life more than food, and the body more than clothing?" (NRSV). He further reminded them that their Heavenly Father knows of their needs. Jesus does not suggest that these matters of life are unimportant nor does he advise laziness. Rather, Jesus suggests that his followers can have calm trust in the providential care of God. This kind of trust is difficult when our world seems to be falling apart.

Jesus' words to those first listeners apply to us as well. Trust in the goodness of God who guides and sustains us and who enables us to remain calm in the face of crisis. God is a loving God who both created the world and continues to uphold it. My dad's faith has been an inspiration to me on this point. He and his family experienced repeated crises when he was a young man. Soon after he married his first wife, a flu epidemic spread through his family. In a matter of several months, eight family members died. On his wife's side of the family, those who died included her mother, father, and brother. Dad then lost his own father, a brother, his newborn baby, and then his wife.

Dad never talked much about that period of his life, but he did respond graciously to our questions. Prior to his death, he and I were alone, riding in my car. As I recall, we were talking about his longtime friend who had just died. I asked him about his grief over the death of his family members when he was a young man. Then I asked how he had lived through such tragedy. With tears in his eyes and with a shaky voice, he said simply, "Trust in God." Those three words contained the secret of Dad's granite-like strength in the face of calamity.

In a matter-of-fact way, Dad was saying that God is a loving God who both created the world and continues to uphold it. He knew by experience that his belief in the providence of God was not a cheap promise that all hardships and difficulties would be smoothed away. Dad knew that Christians are not promised an escape from tragedy.

We can say with certainty that God understands the pain, the grief, the agony we experience during a crisis. Jesus Christ experienced the agony of grief when his friend Lazarus died. Jesus also experienced the pain and humiliation of the cross. He can identify with our pain because he has been there himself and shared it. That's the message of Good Friday.

But God in Jesus Christ did more than just identify with us in his suffering. The message doesn't end with Good Friday; the message ends with Easter.[6] God allows evil to exist in the world. That's the dark side of life. But God in Jesus Christ brought light to all who would receive it. God allows suffering and identified with our suffering by allowing Jesus to die on the cross. The mysterious truth of the cross is that God redeemed us from our sins and from a sinful world through the suffering and death of Christ. The mysterious truth of the resurrection is God's final answer to the problem of suffering. The presence of evil contradicts all that we believe about God's love and power and goodness. Our answer is not an explanation but rather a confession of our faith: "Jesus Christ is risen!" "He is risen indeed!" Jesus was the victim of evil as he suffered and died. Thanks be to God that because of the resurrection, God is victorious over death and suffering. No matter how painful our family crisis, God is stronger! God is the Victor!

You may be thinking, "If God is so strong, why does God let my family suffer?" I cannot answer that question, for I do not know the mind of God. I can say that God allowed God's Son, Jesus Christ, to die on the cross. This same cross was a stumbling block for the early Jews because they believed that a good God would not let the anointed Messiah suffer pain and humiliation. But God and Jesus were vindicated in the resurrection. God did not abandon Jesus on the cross! God's power was present on the cross and in the resurrection. That same power is available to us as we face a crisis.

For our belief about God to be translated into strength, we must approach our crisis realistically. We live in a world of pain and suffering. God's only Son was not exempt from this pain. The dark power of suffering is still at work in the world in which we live. Let us view our crises through Easter morning faith. The empty tomb is a reminder of the power of God who "has rescued us from the power of darkness and transferred us into the kingdom of his beloved Son" (Col 1:13, NRSV).[7]

Simply understanding what the Bible says about the providence of God does not immediately change how we feel about our circumstances. Our goal is to clarify feelings and thoughts as well as our response to the crisis. Clarifying our understanding and belief about God's providence can be one way of affecting our feelings and our response to crisis.

Personal Learning Activity

1. Based on the previous material, write a brief definition of the providence of God.

_____

_____

_____

_____

_____

2. Think of how the death and resurrection of Jesus made a difference in a crisis your family has experienced. Write your thoughts here.

_____

_____

_____

_____

_____

FINDING HOPE WHEN ALL SEEMS HOPELESS

How can we find hope when all seems hopeless? A phrase from an old hymn by Edward Mote sums up where we are headed in regard to hope: "My hope is built on nothing less than Jesus' blood and righteousness."[8] Those words may sound shallow and offer little hope at first, but they are powerful. Let's walk together toward the genuine hope provided by Jesus Christ.

Christian hope is more than optimism for the future. Early in the twentieth century, theologians maintained that, through the goodness of humanity, society was getting better and better and would eventually become a kind of utopia. However, two world wars, numerous lesser wars, and other atrocities destroyed reliance on the goodness of humanity as our ultimate hope.

Christian hope is not gained by denying the world in which we live. Some extremists in Christianity see the world as so evil that they try to remove themselves from it. It is also possible to be so focused on the future as to deny the real world in which we live. Paul and other first-century Christians looked forward to the imminent return of Christ, but Paul also reminded some not to stand "gazing into the sky." We too are guilty of this same kind of gazing if we deny our pain to the point that we focus only on the future. Biblical Christianity looks toward the future with anticipation while remaining vitally related to this world. Jesus did not deny the world; rather, he sought to transform the world. God is still in the business of helping us transform hurts and pains, sorrows and sadness, into purpose for living in the present and hoping for the future.

Christian hope has Jesus Christ as its foundation, the Bible as its textbook, and the purpose of God as its end. Our hope is built on the strongest foundation of all, Jesus Christ. Our hope is not built on the sandcastles of wishful thinking or advanced rational thinking. When crises of life roll in like waves during a storm, only the hope built on the foundation of Jesus Christ will survive. This hope promises a bright future but also gives purpose for the present. Through it we gain what the Bible calls abundant life.

Christian life is bound up in God's revelation of God's self and in God's work through us. It is not something we possess or something we can achieve on our own. Though we do our part, as Morris Ashcraft says in the book, *The Christian Hope*, "human grace is born in response to God's marvelous grace."[9] Christian hope is the genuine human response to God's great gifts to us.

Authentic hope is a divine-human collaboration. It is God's invention, God's creation, but it is something in which we participate. A widow who raised six sons was asked her secret of bringing up such exceptional young men almost entirely on her own. She replied that it wasn't entirely on her own, that God helped and that it had taken a lot of grit and grace. "How's that?" the questioner asked. She replied, "Every night I knelt in prayer and told Him I would furnish the grit if He would furnish the grace."[10] We can count on God to collaborate with us in bringing about hope when we face a family or personal crisis.

One way God works for our good is by transforming us, using the crisis to help us grow as individuals and as families. A key ingredient in moving beyond a crisis relates to our attitude toward life and toward the crisis. Our attitude positively or negatively affects how we deal with a crisis. A negative attitude negatively affects the way in which we deal with a crisis and sometimes aggravates an already bad situation. A positive outlook, on the other hand, helps us deal with a crisis and has the potential to reduce the harmful effects of the crisis. God can join us in our crises at the point of our attitude.

God does not change our attitude against our will, but participates with us in transforming our attitude if we are willing.

We must first be open with God. We need not try to hide our negative attitude. Rather, we should openly share our inmost feelings. Do you blame God for your crisis? Then pray to God, confessing this blame. Are you angry with God for your family's situation? Then confess this anger. Just as the Bible encourages us not to let the sun go down on our anger in relation to other people, we should not allow this to occur between us and God. God has room to accomplish God's transforming work within us to the extent that we are honest and straightforward with God.

As a teenager, I struggled with my faith in God and my blame of God for the crises I faced. I wished I had not faced certain situations in life and sometimes felt cheated by God. I played a game with myself and with others as I used pious language. Many years later, while involved in a small group discussion in a seminary class, I realized that my suppression of hurt had developed into resentment and anger. Toward the end of the class, we were asked to write an evaluation for each class member. We were then allowed to give this open and honest feedback to our classmates. Dr. Larry McSwain, one of the two professors in the class, spoke challenging and penetrating words as he said to me, "John, you are an angry person." Internally I bristled at his words. Verbally I responded, "I'm really not angry."

As I thought about Dr. McSwain's confrontation, I realized that what I had hidden from myself was apparent to others. I was angry at the world and maybe even angry at God. I pondered this as I drove to the community where I was pastor and where my wife and I lived. Later that evening I made a list of more than a dozen major issues and events in my life that caused me anger.

In our next class period, I asked for time to share this list with my classmates. I also committed to them and to myself that I would seek a counselor with whom to vent my anger and sort through my hurt. My attitude of anger, which grew from crises I faced as a teenager and went suppressed for years, was controlling my relationship to myself, my relationship to others, and my relationship to God.

It so happened that Dr. Andrew Lester was the other professor in this seminary class. He had written and studied extensively about the source and cure of anger. He agreed to walk with me in a series of formal counseling sessions to help me deal with my reservoir of anger. I was enabled through his careful guidance to vent the anger, confess it to God, and move beyond it. This did not occur instantly; rather, it was a lengthy process involving the participation of God, Dr. Lester, and me. Dr. Lester facilitated the process of growth through actively listening to my struggles, walking through these hurts with me, and providing feedback. The sessions also required much soul searching and hard work on my part. Through it all, we collaborated with God in the process, and my attitude was transformed. As this transformation took place, my entire outlook on life changed.

Recently, years after the above incident, I was the counselor helping a couple find hope in their marriage. One evening, Cricket made an insightful analogy regarding counseling. Her husband, Jerry, had taken it upon himself to build shelves in their closet. The closet was cluttered with no shelves, and while Cricket was away at a conference, Jerry took everything out of the closet, piling it in the corner of their bedroom, and began building shelves. Cricket returned home and was surprised to see all the clutter but grateful Jerry had taken the initiative to build much-needed shelves. She said of this situation, "After Jerry has finished building the shelves, I hope we don't just throw all of our things back in the closet. I think we need to sort things out, keeping some things and throwing other things away. I think we need to organize those things we keep." She went on to make the comparison to counseling. "What I'd like from counseling is to sort out everything. Our lives have become like that junky closet. I hope we can throw some things away, keep some important things, but more than anything sort out the clutter."

Whether we talk to a trusted friend, counselor, or pastor, it may be important to find someone to help us sort out the clutter brought about by a crisis. Hope is reborn as we begin to fit the pieces back together and find wholeness and peace.

I believe God seldom changes us instantaneously, making all things immediately work together for our good. Rather, God uses our internal will and strength and the wisdom and assistance of those around us, participating with us in the process. The key is our willingness to face our attitudes and beliefs squarely, whether positive or negative. Again, like the man Jesus encountered after the transfiguration, we confess, "Lord, I believe; help my unbelief." When we respond in this fashion, I suspect Jesus will respond to us the way he responded to this man. Jesus did not chasten him; rather, he lovingly accepted his confession of doubt mixed with faith and healed the man's son.

Jesus Christ can take the faith and hope we have, feeble as it may be, and collaborate with us in making it genuine. We hand him our hope, even though it may look more like wishful thinking than genuine hope, and we confess our hurt to him. Sometimes we sort through our multifaceted pain with a trusted counselor. Eventually, God transforms our hopelessness and our superficial hope into genuine hope.

Victor Frankl lived through some of the worst atrocities ever known. An Austrian psychiatrist, he survived the Nazi concentration camps of Auschwitz and Dachau. He was totally stripped of his humanity, and he watched as thousands were taken to their deaths. Almost every member of his immediate family perished in the gas chambers, including his father, mother, brother, and wife; only a sister survived. Frankl observed his fellow prisoners as they fought hopelessness and despair. He discovered that when a prisoner could find some kind of hope for a future outside the prison—when the prisoner could find meaning in life—the prisoner won the battle over despair.

Frankl survived the inhumanity of the camps. From his experiences, he founded a school of psychiatry known as Logotherapy. Briefly, logotherapy says that when a person can find meaning in life, that person can find hope. Through various methods, the logotherapist works with a person, helping him or her discover a higher meaning to life.

I've just read Frankl's book about his experiences in the concentration camps and about his founding of logotherapy. Several things come to mind as I reflect on what I've read. First, my family crises, though real and painful, pale when compared to what thousands of individuals and families faced during the Holocaust. This has not made me feel better because others underwent worse suffering. Rather, it has helped me gain perspective on the family crises I've experienced.

My second response relates to the search for meaning and hope. Frankl was fond of quoting the philosopher Nietzsche, who said, "He who has a why to live can bear with almost any how."[11] In other words, the person (or family) who can discover a purpose, a deeper meaning to life, can bear almost any circumstance, no matter how dreadful, no matter how traumatic.

When we think in ultimate terms, God, our heavenly Father as revealed in Jesus Christ, is the ultimate meaning in this life and the next. We have the possibility of knowing and experiencing this meaning through Jesus Christ. God in Jesus Christ transforms our meaninglessness into meaning, our hopelessness into genuine hope.

GOD HELPS US DISCOVER A HOPEFUL FUTURE

As a pastoral counselor now, I regularly help people deal with the crises of life. I sometimes use what is known as cognitive therapy. One view used in cognitive therapy is that we cannot directly change our feelings, but we can change our cognition, that is, our cognitive interpretation of events. A colleague, Dr. Wade Rowatt, suggests that when something happens, we have thoughts about this event and our thoughts come about because of our internal dictionary. This internal dictionary has been formed over the years by our education and also by our experiences.

Our internal dictionary affects not only our immediate response to a crisis but also our future story—the story we have in our heads about what might happen.

Dr. Andrew Lester's book, *Hope in Pastoral Care and Counseling*,[12] has greatly informed my thinking regarding hope. To review again what I stated in the preface, Lester's book on hope is about story, particularly future story. Let me explain by first telling of a recent experience.

Not long ago I spilled coffee in my wife's new car while she was out of town. Connie's rule is, "No eating or drinking in my car." Quick to find a solution to my carelessness, I went to the local home store to purchase carpet-cleaning supplies. I rushed to the checkout, stopped abruptly, and quickly reached for my money. The cashier had a startled look on her face that seemed to say, "What's going on with this goofy guy?" I responded to her nonverbal comment by saying, "Everybody has a story; do you want to hear mine?" She did and we both laughed about my predicament.

The fact is that everybody has at least three stories. The first relates to our past. The second relates to our current situation. The third relates to our future.

Remembering certain stories of our past can trigger anger, hurt, and pain. Our current issues can cause a narrow focus on our present pain or problems. Edwin Friedman and other family systems therapists use a term called "transgenerational residue." The term means what it implies; there is a lasting residue in my life that was transmitted from previous generations. My past story is made up of things I remember and things I don't consciously know about, such as issues passed on to me by previous generations.

While the past may haunt us and the present may consume us, our real energy lies in our future story. All of us tend to live toward our future story, whether that story is negative or positive, hopeful or despairing.

Everyone has a future story, and we're living toward it whether it tells of despair or of hope. Some time ago, I had a conversation with a pastor who led an inner-city congregation. The people in that neighborhood, for the most part, lived in poverty. Over time, this congregation focused their ministry on youth in their community. One particularly bright young person began to stand out. This young lady had the grades to go to college and thus break the cycle of despair and poverty. Adult leaders in this congregation helped her apply to college and also for scholarships, for without significant financial assistance she would not be able to attend. She was accepted and awarded the kinds of scholarships that made college attendance possible. But when the time came for her to go away to college, she decided she couldn't leave home. She said she simply could not picture herself leaving her community and entering college. Her future story was confined to her current circumstances.

I think one of the greatest examples of how this worked is the story of the exodus. Moses had led the people of God from bondage in Egypt toward a promised land. God's mighty power had helped the people break the bonds of slavery. God's guidance had led Moses and the people through the desert toward this new land. It was now time to send spies into the land. According to Scripture (Num 13–14), Moses was to choose twelve men, one from each tribe, to scout out the land and discover the vulnerabilities. Upon their return, ten of the spies said it would be impossible to overtake this land due to the size of the men and the greatness of their armaments: "So they brought to the Israelites an unfavorable report of the land that they had spied out, saying, 'The land that we have gone through as spies is a land that devours its inhabitants; and all the people that we saw in it are of great size . . . and to ourselves we seemed like grasshoppers, and so we seemed to them'" (Num 13:32-33, NRSV).

Joshua and Caleb, on the other hand, brought a far different report. They said, "The land that we went through as spies is an exceedingly good land. If the LORD is pleased with us, he will bring us into this land and give it to us, a land that flows with milk and honey. Only, do not rebel against the LORD; and do not fear the people of the land, for they are no more than bread for us; their protection is removed from them, and the LORD is with us; do not fear them" (Num 14:7-9, NRSV).

How you view life—how you view a crisis—makes all the difference in the world. Caleb and Joshua's view was that a new world was open to their people; all they had to do was enter. There was no reason to fear. The ten unnamed spies, however, could only see the threat and were therefore paralyzed from moving forward.

These early followers of God responded negatively to a grand opportunity. As modern descendants of these people, we sometimes waver on the precipice of challenging opportunities that call us to God's future. The story of the spies is a story of the future and how it is interpreted. A dozen men went into a new and strange land. Ten gave a negative report. They talked about the impossibilities. Two gave a positive report. They talked about the possibilities. Ten couldn't imagine stepping into the promised future because they were paralyzed by fear. Two couldn't imagine shrinking back from this promised new world.

What is your future story? How does your future story compare with the future story God has for you? The following Scripture passages may help you determine God's future story for you: Jeremiah 29:11; Numbers 13:1-3, 25-33; 14:6-10. Consider the following applications to your life situation as you recall a specific crisis.

• God has plans for us that are hopeful. Our well-being is a top concern of God.
• When our present and future seem filled with giants, Joshua and Caleb remind us that we can conquer the giants (because God is on our side).
• God walks with us into our future. The future belongs to God.
• God is interested in our past and also in our current situation, but perhaps God is more interested in helping us claim our hopeful future story.

We end our discussion about hope where we began:

My hope is built on nothing less
Than Jesus' blood and righteousness;
I dare not trust the sweetest frame,
But wholly lean on Jesus' name.

When darkness seems to hide His face,
I rest on His unchanging grace;
In every high and stormy gale,
My anchor holds within the veil.

On Christ, The solid Rock, I stand;
All other ground is sinking sand,
All other ground is sinking sand. (Edward Mote)

A family crisis often feels like a stormy gale in which Christ's face seems hidden from us. Even so, we can count on his unchanging grace to transform our future stories of despair into future stories of hope. We can find genuine hope in the ultimate meaning of life, namely, Jesus Christ.

Personal Learning Activity

1. Explain the meaning of the following sentence: "He who has a why to live can bear with almost any how."

_____

_____

_____

2. How has your faith in Jesus Christ helped you discover a deeper meaning to life?

_____

_____

_____

3. With whom do you identify most—the ten spies who felt like grasshoppers or Joshua and Caleb who saw the possibilities? How can you begin to reconstruct your future story to think of the possibilities?

_____

_____

_____

SUMMARY

Crisis brings a sense of hopelessness and meaninglessness. Beliefs that we once accepted at face value are now challenged. In this chapter, our goal has been to face this challenge squarely and to avoid the two extremes of denying hope or denying our suffering. We have sought to make sense of our suffering while considering the meaning of the providence of God as it relates to our crisis. We have moved toward hope in the face of hopelessness. We have looked at how our future story can provide energy that moves us forward into positive ways.

Crisis does not occur in a vacuum. In the next chapter, we look more closely at how families function before and during a crisis. This will further help us in our effort to understand our own family and how we can respond creatively to a family crisis.

NOTES

1. C. S. Lewis, *The Problem of Pain* (London: Fontana Books, 1961) 77.

2. Epicurus, quoted in L. D. Johnson, *The Morning After Death* (Nashville: Broadman Press, 1978) 102.

3. Harry Emerson Fosdick, *Living Under Tension* (New York: Harper and Brothers, 1941) 218.

4. Ibid., 218–19.

5. Georgia Harkness, *The Providence of God* (New York: Abingdon, 1960) 17.

6. Shirley C. Gutherie, Jr., *Christian Doctrine: Teachings of the Christian Church* (Richmond: CLC Press, 1968) 182ff.

7. Ibid., 183.

8. Edward Mote, "The Solid Rock," Convention Press, 1991, used by permission.

9. Morris Ashcraft, *The Christian Hope*, vol. 15 of *The Layman's Library of Christian Doctrine* (Nashville: Broadman, 1968) 23.

10. Jim N. Griffith, *Sure You Can* (Nashville: Broadman, 1978) 108.

11. Quoted in Frankl's book, *Man's Search for Meaning* (New York: Pocket Books, 1959) xi.

12. Andrew D. Lester, *Hope in Pastoral Care and Counseling* (Louisville KY: Westminster John Knox Press, 1995).

Chapter 3

FAMILIES FUNCTIONING BEFORE
AND DURING A CRISIS

And when he [Jesus] was twelve years old, they went up as usual for the festival.
. . . When they did not find him, they returned to Jerusalem to search for him.
After three days they found him in the temple, sitting among the teachers, listen-
ing to them and asking them questions . . . . Then he went down with them and
came to Nazareth, and was obedient to them. (Luke 2:42, 45, 46, 51a, NRSV)

How does your family respond to crisis? Notice the question focuses on the
family and not the individual. This may be a difficult question to answer
because we usually think in terms of how individual family members
respond to a crisis. It may be easier to think about how a parent or a child
responds. It is quite another matter to consider how our family responds to a
given crisis. Because our focus in this book is on family crisis, let's turn our
thinking to how a family unit might respond in a crisis situation.

The key concept to consider when thinking about a family crisis is relationship. When talking about a crisis an individual faces, we think about
what is happening within the person. We might ask, "What is this person
feeling, thinking, desiring?" When talking about a family crisis, we look at
what is going on within an individual and add the dimension of relationships. One way to gain a better understanding of a family crisis is to ask,
"What's going on between family members?"

The important feature of a family crisis is the relationships that exist
between family members. As we think about family relationships and family
response to crisis, let's look first at our assumptions about families and how
they operate. Clarifying our assumptions will help us get a clearer picture of
what happens between family members.[1]

1. The family is more than the sum of individual family members. A
family has qualities that cannot be understood simply by combining the
family members' individual personalities. From this point of view, we look
beyond individual family members to the ways in which a family relates,
communicates, and solves problems. Recognizing these patterns helps us
understand how families operate and specifically how they respond to a
crisis.

2. Families develop unique patterns of response. Beginning with the parents' courtship and marriage, a family develops certain ways of dealing with day-to-day life. These patterns include, among other things, who has the right to make decisions, how differences of opinion are handled, and how emotions can be expressed.

3. Some family patterns are constructive while other patterns are destructive. Families have an amazing capacity for creativity and also a remarkable capacity for destruction. The patterns of relationships within the family (more than just individual personalities) determine the family's destructive or constructive characteristics.

Now that we understand three basic assumptions about families, let's take a closer look at how families operate.

UNDERSTANDING HOW FAMILIES WORK

Family systems theory helps us understand how families function from day-to-day and also how they cope during a crisis. Just as each individual has a personality, each family has its own personality traits. The following are characteristics most families possess.

Families Move Toward Balance

Visualize a family as a hanging mobile. When one part of the mobile is moved or blown by the wind, the other parts must move for the mobile to regain balance. When a family member becomes ill, gets in trouble with the law, gets a promotion, or has a baby, the family becomes imbalanced. When this occurs, other family members compensate. The change, whether good or bad, creates an imbalance that, in turn, causes other family members to try to restore the equilibrium.[2]

The family of Jesus experienced a minor crisis when he was left behind at the temple. Think of the family imbalance brought about by this situation. The Gospel of Luke (2:41-52) describes how Jesus went with his family to Jerusalem at the age of twelve to observe the Passover. When the feast ended, his parents went a day's journey without Jesus, thinking he was with friends or other family members. When they did not find him, the Scripture indicates that they rushed about looking for him among their kinsmen and acquaintances. Realizing he must have been left behind in Jerusalem, they returned to the city, only to search for three days before finding him.

Imagine their feelings as they rushed from place to place looking for their son. To say the least, a missing family member brought their family out of balance. They must have breathed a sigh of relief when they found him. With all family members now back together, the Scripture says they returned home. Balance was regained.

Families Develop Rules

Whether written or spoken, secret or open, families live by "family rules." These rules govern the behavior and the relationships of family members. "Rules are a set of expectations about how people should conduct themselves in various kinds of settings and circumstances. Rules say what is allowable and not allowable. They also say what the consequences are when the rules are obeyed or disobeyed."[3]

Sometimes rules are spoken. Other times they are unspoken. A spoken rule in my family of origin was not to talk back to parents. Other examples of spoken rules are common manners like wash before you eat, don't talk with your mouth full, and don't interrupt when someone else is talking.

Unspoken rules are a bit trickier. Family members may understand and even agree on these rules without openly acknowledging them. An unspoken rule in my family of origin was, "It's better to remain silent when wronged than speak up and risk getting angry." The rule was never said, but family members were aware of its existence. We were also aware of the assumption upon which the rule was based, which was itself a rule, namely, "It's not okay to be angry." Family members were expected to be agreeable at all times. I'm not suggesting that we were always agreeable; I'm saying this was the rule.

In other families, conflict is the norm. In these cases, the rule might be, "Arguments are better than indifference; one's care is shown through strong emotion."[4]

Rules are important to the daily routine of families because they help family members know what is acceptable and unacceptable behavior. A crisis brings about an interruption or disruption of the rules. Families in crisis search for new rules or seek to regain the old rules.

Families Develop Hierarchies

Hierarchies, structures of authority, evolve so that families have a way of making decisions and accomplishing tasks. In this way, the family avoids chaos and unpredictability. The norm for families is for the older generation to have authority over the younger. The worth of this biblical principle is generally accepted by family therapists; that is, within healthy families, power is securely in the hands of the parents. For healthy families, this power is not heavy-handed but rather provides a kind of easy leadership. If not based on anger or conflict, a generation gap between parents and children is natural and desired.

Some families are rigid in their hierarchical structure. Other families are less rigid. In any case, when a crisis occurs, this structure is thrown off balance. Flexibility regarding authority is the key to coping successfully. Families that are not flexible to changes have great difficulty coping when a crisis upends family structures.

In some cases, rigidity not only contributes to an existing crisis, but it can precipitate a crisis. The latter is especially true regarding parent-teen issues. Adolescence means change, and in order for everyone to experience this period with relative harmony, parents need a degree of flexibility as they change in response to the adolescent's changing. Charles Swindoll makes this point in his book titled *Growing Wise in Family Life*:

> When it comes to rearing teenagers rigidity is lethal. Parents who refuse to flex, who insist on everything remaining exactly as it was in earlier years can expect their kids to rebel. But parents who are secure and mature enough to give ground, provide space, allow room, listen more than lecture, release tight control, maintain a calm and affirming attitude, and good sense of humor can look forward to some of the most invigorating and adventuresome years in all of life.[5]

Rigidity can also apply to a family's overall response to a crisis. A family can be "stuck in one gear" as they respond to crisis. When this single response fails, the family is unable to adapt. Inability to have a flexible response leads to increasing fragmentation for a rigid family.

Families Tend to Develop Emotional Triangles

An emotional triangle is any three-way relationship. A triangle can center on people and/or issues. Emotional triangles evolve in families and relationships as a way of coping with stress. When the tension increases, another person or issue is pulled in to reduce the tension. For example, two parents and a child; parents and a child's misbehavior; a husband and wife and his/her drinking problem; a husband and wife and his work; or a husband and wife and a family crisis.[6]

A biblical example of a family triangle is reflected in the family of Jacob. Genesis 27 describes how Jacob's mother, Rebekah, schemed with him to obtain his father's blessing that was rightfully Esau's. The Bible describes how Isaac sent Jacob to live with Laban, Rebekah's brother. Jacob met his match in Laban. Through the deception of Laban, Jacob married Leah when he thought he was marrying Rachel. The Bible again shows how a triangle develops with Jacob and his two wives, Leah and Rachel.

The more modern, but classic, example of a triangle is the husband who is dissatisfied with his wife and their relationship and thus gets involved in an extramarital affair. Television soap operas thrive on such triangles.

Another example is when a child "triangles" with a parent in order to gain power over the other parent. The child tries to get one parent to take sides about a particular issue.

Somewhat mysteriously, triangles sometimes come about as a way of getting the focus off a particularly stressful issue. For example, a couple may focus on a child's misbehavior in order to avoid dealing with their own relational problems. This triangle may temporarily ease the tension between the parents, but eventually it only complicates the family's problems.

A crisis, while painful and traumatic in itself, can serve to draw attention away from other family problems. A man who had been married for fifteen years reported to his minister that he was seriously contemplating divorce. He reported knowing from the beginning that the marriage seemed doomed for failure. The marriage had begun and was continually characterized by a stormy relationship.

Soon after the couple married, the wife became pregnant and had their first child. The child had physical problems that required medical attention. After this crisis ended, the family faced another crisis, and then another. The crises seemed strung together, lasting all their married life. By diverting their attention away from their stormy relationship, the crises served to keep them together. But the couple's togetherness was not an intimate closeness because they were focused on the third corner of the triangle, namely, the current crisis. Then one day the crises ceased. At this point, the man reported that it became frightfully apparent that their relationship had no depth. An extremely stormy period followed, and the marriage faltered.

This is an example of how triangles temporarily ease or absorb tension in family relationships. In the long run, however, triangles serve to increase family problems.

Families Develop a Particular Closeness/Distance Barometer

Some families are so close and dependent on each other that they seem stuck together. Family specialists call this being fused or enmeshed. These family members are so close, in fact, that it is difficult for individual family members to identify their personal feelings. They have difficulty thinking of self and only see the "we" of the family.

In other families, members are more distant from one another. One lady reported to her church group that her family of origin felt cold and indifferent. She said it wasn't that they were hostile toward one another, but that they expressed neither positive nor negative feelings toward one another. They lived in the same house, but it was as if they lived in different worlds.

Extreme distance or extreme closeness can intensify an existing crisis or even cause a crisis. Families that are so close that they are fused or stuck together may collapse or blow apart during a crisis because none are strong enough to withstand the crisis. Distant family members do not have it much better because they are cut off from the emotional support their family could provide.

Personal Learning Activity

Review the five general characteristics of families:

1. Families move toward balance.
2. Families develop rules.
3. Families develop hierarchies.
4. Families tend to develop emotional triangles.
5. Families develop a particular closeness/distance barometer.

Using these five general characteristics of families, write a paragraph describing your family. Of the five characteristics mentioned, which most mirrors your family? Which is most unlike your family?

_____

_____

_____

_____

_____

EFFECTS OF CRISIS ON FAMILIES

Family reactions to a crisis are complex. Since each family is unique, a specific response to a given crisis is not precisely predictable. However, family and individual responses to a crisis can generally be anticipated. Being aware of typical responses helps us better understand what is happening and therefore empowers us and enables us to handle crisis more efficiently. The following general responses are suggestive of the ones families often make to crises.

Crisis Brings Change

The most pervasive effect of a crisis on families is change. Life is full of changes, but crisis hastens the process of change. Depending on the situation, change may be short lived or long term. Developmental crises bring changes at a more relaxed pace, while acute crises bring immediate changes. Crises related to disaster-related or social crises may bring both immediate and long-lasting changes. In any case, a family crisis brings changes in roles, responsibilities, and, sometimes lifestyles.

The hospitalization of a family member may cause a temporary shift in roles. For example, if the mother is hospitalized, the father or even an older child may find it necessary to assume some of her former responsibilities, such as cooking, buying groceries, and caring for younger children. As mentioned earlier, family members change in order to bring a sense of balance and stability back to the family.

I recall a distinct and lasting shift in roles when Mother died. Whereas Dad had always been helpful with household chores, his primary role was that of provider. Upon Mother's death, he became both homemaker and provider. I remember having a family meeting in which we discussed who would be responsible for certain household chores. Dishwashing was the least favorite of my two brothers, ages twelve and nine, and me. Dad accepted this task while I became the chief cook and my two brothers accepted other chores. With Mother's death, our roles changed permanently.

In addition to role shifts, crisis can bring about dramatic changes in lifestyle. One occasion when such changes occur follows divorce. Divorce typically involves dramatic changes in economic status, living arrangements, parental responsibilities, and household responsibilities. One person may continue to live in the same house or apartment previously occupied by the couple, while the other must make separate housing arrangements. The parent with custodial rights must often make childcare arrangements not previously necessary. Many men may initially experience considerable difficulty in maintaining a household routine. Previously unemployed women may find it necessary to work, and divorced fathers may expand their workload to increase income in order to afford child support payments.

Change is the one common denominator of all family crises. Like it or not, crisis brings changes to families. Some changes are small, while others are disruptive. With the crisis, families are forced to make adjustments.

Crisis Disrupts Family Routine

When crisis comes home, a family's routine is disrupted. Families in crisis often feel as if they are living life on hold. The disruption that takes place during an acute crisis may be more intense during certain phases of the crisis. For example, hospitalization of a family member may disrupt the family routine more than the time that follows hospitalization. The death of a family member may cause immediate disruption of the family routine. This disruption may subside after the funeral and gradually taper off during the next weeks and months as the family regains its routine or shifts to another routine.

For months prior to the death of Connie's mother, our family routine changed. On occasion we altered vacation or holiday plans in order to be with Mrs. Jackson. At other times, Connie took sick leave from work in order to care for her mother. During these times, the children and I found our routine changing to accommodate Connie's absence. Each of us was glad to make adjustments, but we all longed for the day when our routine would get back to normal.

Crisis Limits Control

To one degree or another, a crisis leaves families out of control. A crisis causes us to lose control over people, relationships, and events. It's as if the crisis controls our lives.

Life must go on and daily choices must be made, but the crisis often governs our decisions. Some things are totally unavoidable. Who, for example, can control the ferocious power of a tornado? Other crises may not totally eliminate our control; however, our love for family members may leave us with little choice but to drop what we are doing and provide help.

A middle-aged Sunday school teacher relates how his family visited his parents' home for Thanksgiving. His father's condition with Alzheimer's disease worsened, and his mother was becoming weary as she cared for him. As is often the case with those who suffer with Alzheimer's disease, the father's personality changed as his memory deteriorated. He required constant attention because he was not capable of taking care of his needs. The son, a committed Christian, expressed his intense frustration and helplessness as he observed his father's declining condition and his mother's struggle to provide care. "The issue for me," he said, "is loss of control. I struggle with this issue, but I know in my heart that God is still in control. So I place my faith and trust in God." Control is an issue families face as crisis comes home.

Crisis Triggers Disturbing Emotions

Crisis often triggers unpleasant emotions. These emotions may include anxiety, guilt, regret, and anger. Such feelings can catch us by surprise as we experience emotions we didn't know we had or that may have been dormant. These emotions are often frightening and uncomfortable.

Guilt is a common emotion triggered during a crisis. Depending on the situation, a person may regret having done or said something to an ill or deceased family member. At other times, guilt may come about as a result of a failed relationship.

Recently I spoke with a close friend whose dad had to be hospitalized because of a near-death illness. My friend had traveled to a neighboring state to be with his father and other family members. I listened as he told me the details of the illness and how they waited in the intensive care waiting room for several days and were still unsure of his father's future. He told how other family members were doing and of his father's courage during this emergency. I then asked about my friend's well-being. "You've told me about the others. How are you feeling?"

His response went something like this: "I'm doing fine now, but if it hadn't been for a conversation Dad and I had a few weeks ago, I would be a basket case." He then described how his conversation with his father had helped mend their strained relationship. The conversation had been a time of reconciliation. Since I knew this person well, I said, "I know you are thankful you had that conversation. I would imagine your father's near-death experience kicked up enough feelings as it was." He responded, "You are right about that." We were both reminded of the fact that feelings of guilt and regret are often stirred in times of crisis.

Other emotions that surface during a family crisis are anger, anxiety, and fear. It is easy to become angry with somebody or even with God for causing our distress. Fear of the unknown is heightened. An overall anxious feeling is common.

We can experience a vicious cycle of negative feelings, becoming angry with ourselves for having such negative thoughts and feelings. Because our ideal is not to have these feelings, we may feel guilty for possessing them. During these times, we need to remember that we cannot always control our feelings. God created our feelings for a purpose. When we have such feelings, we can depend on God to see us through. Christian friends or a pastor can help us sort through these feelings.

Families who have rules against sharing feelings tend to have more difficulty moving beyond a crisis. Christians may be particularly vulnerable at this point. One's belief may prevent the person or family from admitting that certain negative feelings exist.

An elderly minister, well past the age of retirement, continued in an active pastorate partly for financial reasons. He and his wife were overwhelmed when the church terminated him. With a lot of tenacity and some denial, he maintained what he described as a strong faith in God. He had difficulty discussing his anger related to the people and particularly his anger related to God. His wife became depressed during this time. Part of the dynamic in their relationship was that any time she moved toward expressing negative emotion, he began cheering her up by talking only about the positive results of the termination. His belief that Christians should not be angry, particularly toward God, did not allow him to give his wife permission to express these emotions. Added to this was his intense desire to take care of his wife. Not realizing or admitting that each person must work through his or her own feelings, he tried to take care of his wife by telling her what she ought to feel. This, of course, did not work. His refusal to allow her to discuss her deep negative feelings further aggravated her depression and also the family crisis.

When there is an internal prohibition against certain feelings, denial often results. Families or family members who deny the existence of a crisis tend to have a difficult time growing as a result of a crisis. How can one deal with a crisis that he or she has denied? Sometimes the actual crisis is not denied but rather one's feelings related to the crisis. Here again, Christians may be particularly susceptible to this way of coping. Denial can offer a temporary easing of tension, but the long-term effect is further aggravation of the crisis.

Denial or avoidance keeps us from squarely facing the crisis at hand. For example, one coping strategy related to grief is to keep busy. While it is important for the bereaved to return to a normal routine, this strategy can lengthen the grieving process. This happens when keeping busy becomes a diversionary tactic that helps the grieving person avoid thinking about the loss and suppresses feelings of anxiety and grief. Keeping busy by returning to or finding worthwhile tasks to perform and worthwhile work to do can be therapeutic. However, this kind of behavior becomes dysfunctional when it is the primary method of coping and when it serves the purpose of denying reality.

Crisis Alters Communication Patterns

Increased stress brought about by a crisis changes the way a family communicates. The family may depend on a certain member as a link in receiving and sharing information. If this person is hospitalized or permanently absent, the patterns of communication are strained and must be altered in response to the crisis.

Families often have unspoken rules about how and even whether information is shared with other family members. Under normal circumstances and concerning most subjects, a family might be open with one another. A crisis forces a family to decide how it will handle certain information. For example, how will the family handle the diagnosis of cancer? Will this information be kept from the person with cancer or from part of the family? Will the information be shared with close family members with the condition of not bringing up the subject again? Or will every family member be informed about the diagnosis with permission to discuss this information outside the family?

I know families who have tried to keep a secret from a family member following the diagnosis of cancer or some other dreaded disease. The rationale is to keep the person from worrying. However, this usually has a counterproductive effect. The person from whom the secret is kept often senses something is wrong, but, because of the secrecy surrounding the situation, the person's anxiety is raised. The person is not able to base his or her concern on facts and is instead left to wonder. In cases like this, the secret is almost always revealed and the stress of strained communication adds to the trauma of the disease.

Poor communication further adds to a family's inability to grow through a crisis. Families with poor communication patterns are in danger of regressing as a result of a crisis. Information that is not shared may cause family members to feel left out. These feelings, in turn, trigger more negative emotions such as anger. When information is not shared, perceptions are likely to become misperceptions.

Sometimes family members don't share information because they want to protect others from unpleasant situations. Parents may try to protect children from what they perceive as harsh realities. Care certainly needs to be taken concerning the intensity of information given to small children. In many cases, however, older children are better able to face crisis if they have the facts. Otherwise, they are left to wonder, and what's in their imaginations can become far scarier than the reality.

In my life, my family's poor communication left me unprepared for my mother's death. I became aware only several hours prior to her death that her condition was critical. Years later, I asked my father why I had not been given this information. His response was that he did not want to upset me because he continued to have hope that she would not die. While this may have helped him cope, the poor communication further intensified my grief.

Crisis Causes Time Pressures and Increased Fatigue

When crisis comes home, time pressure on families grows intense. The crisis consumes so much time that normal family obligations lack attention. Sometimes significant life choices must be made in a matter of minutes. Families in crisis add time pressure to their long list of changes brought home by a crisis.

Fatigue is a natural consequence of time pressure. Family members often go without sleep in order to care for others. Because the crisis stimulates bodily functions, families in crisis often initially respond with superhuman strength. But the stimulation quickly wears thin, and fatigue becomes the order of the day for families in crisis.

Personal Learning Activity

Complete the following sentences:

1. The most pervasive effect of crisis on families is _____
_____.

2. A crisis disrupts a family's _____.

3. A crisis causes us to lose control over _____
_____
_____.

4. A crisis triggers disturbing _____.

5. A crisis sometimes alters the _____
_____ patterns of families.

6. Family members experience _____ pressure and increased
_____ during a crisis.

CAPITALIZING ON DIFFERENCES

While we have named general ways families respond to a crisis, each family is unique. For this reason, each family's response to a crisis is unique. Our personalities are different. We sometimes perceive life events differently. We respond differently to a crisis. Sometimes we allow our differences to keep us from making our best response to a crisis. Recognizing and accepting the worth of each family member's uniqueness will help us better cope with a crisis.

An experience of my friends Guy and Nancy Futral reminds me how differently two individuals, though part of the same family, can perceive the world around them. Guy and Nancy enjoy a daily walk as a time of exercise and being together. Some days they walk and talk; some days they simply walk. On a recent walk they began talking after a lengthy silence. On previous days they had noticed a brown circle in a neighbor's otherwise green lawn. As they walked past the yard on this day, Nancy said, "I wonder what's making that ring?" She was looking at a ring-like pattern in the grass. Guy didn't notice the ring in the grass that particular morning but rather heard the ringing of wind chimes on a neighbor's back porch. Surprised that Nancy didn't recognize the noise as coming from the chimes, Guy responded, "Why, it's the chimes!" After only four more steps, Nancy stopped Guy and with his face in her hands said, "Do you hear what I'm saying?" "Yes," Guy replied, "you want to know what's making the ringing noise. It's the wind chimes." Nancy's reply, "No, silly, I'm talking about the ring in the grass; that brown circle in the grass!" Guy tells this with laughter and an observation about their petty misunderstanding. "She sees and I hear. We often experience life differently."

Whether through sight or sound, I suspect members of your family also perceive the world differently. When a family crisis occurs, each family member perceives the crisis differently and has his or her own way of coping. We simply cannot expect or demand uniformity of response to a crisis.

A variety of factors causes us to respond to crisis in different ways. Some of these include age, family or cultural background, and personality. For example, family or cultural background influences the nature of the grief response. Many men were taught as children that "big boys" should not cry. So now as men they remain strong and keep their inner pain to themselves. A man may know it's okay to cry in public, but he may struggle between his bravado and his deep hurt. The social stigma of men and boys crying may not be as prevalent today as in the past. Nevertheless, it still points to one way people experience grief differently.

Personality has a great deal to do with how a person experiences and responds to a crisis. Some people are more outgoing or extroverted in their behavior. That is, they find it easy to talk to someone else about situations. An extrovert gains energy from being with other people. Often, extroverts process their emotions externally—that is, they talk about their feelings. A person who is more inner-directed or introverted gains energy from solitude. Following a loss, the extrovert needs opportunities to verbalize his loss, while the introvert may process his or her feelings inwardly.

Recognizing that each family member is unique and will respond uniquely to a crisis, how shall we deal with our differences? Should we press for uniformity of response, or should we let each person cope in their own way? How can we capitalize on differences?

IT'S OKAY TO BE DIFFERENT

Families need to discover the strength that comes from the uniqueness of each individual. Too often we view our differences as bad. If a person doesn't see things our way, we may think his or her way is inferior. We may see differences as a threat to our personhood or a threat to harmony. We may view family accord as an ideal to be gained in spite of individual views or differences.

What happens in your family when a family member responds in a different manner? Is the family member made to feel strange? We may desire a close-knit family, but being close does not mean each person must think and act the same way.

Families can capitalize on differences, drawing on the strengths of other family members. This can occur when differences are not seen as deficiencies.

Even though we know it is okay to be different, anxiety about differences may cause us to put pressure on other family members to conform. We may perceive the differences as a threat to our personhood or to our ideal of family relationships. Our desire, and sometimes our anxiety, about reaching the ideal in family relationships may cause us to act in ways that hinder us from reaching our ideal.

Pressure to conform in order to bring about harmony can have a counterproductive affect, adding to an existing crisis or even precipitating a new crisis. When differences are not respected, family members respond in one of four basic ways. They comply, rebel, attack, or cut off. The healthier way is to remain close and affirm each other's differences.

Comply

One way families cope with their anxiety about differences is through compliance. This is an effort to maintain balance while avoiding differences. But while it may be a way to maintain balance, it becomes detrimental to a family's ability to deal with crisis.

"Peace at any price" is the motto of a compliant family member. Because the ideal for this person is togetherness or harmony, conflict is avoided at all costs. Though this may be an unconscious action, the compliant person fears conflict because they fear it would bring about separation.

Compliance has the opposite result of what is intended. "Peace at any price" actually brings about distance between family members that keep a family from responding to a crisis productively. For example, a wife may comply with her husband's demands without telling him of her true feelings. Conflict is avoided, but her hidden feelings of hostility create distance in their relationship.

Rebel

A second response to pressure for conformity is rebellion. Rebels appear to want distance and independence, but because complete independence is too scary the rebellious person stays close and rebels.

The rebel defines his or her "differentness" by doing the opposite of what the authority figure expects. Often, the authority not only tells the rebel what to do but bails out the rebel when he or she fails. When this happens, the rebel doesn't have to bear the consequences of his or her actions, thus the rebellious behavior is reinforced. Both the authority and the rebel enable this pattern of behavior to repeat itself. As you might imagine, a family crisis can be the result.

Attack/Blame

Attackers deal with differences by blaming. The attacker tries to change the other person by whatever means possible. Conflict is the order of the day, particularly when two or more family members are attackers.

People engaged in such struggle identify the problem as being with the other person. This can become a vicious cycle as each person thinks the other person must change in order to achieve progress. An example of such cyclical behavior might be a husband's drinking and a wife's nagging. She may blame her nagging on his drinking and he may blame his drinking on her nagging. The impossible situation becomes a never-ending cycle of hostility because each person blames the situation on the other.

Families in crisis sometimes deny the real source of the crisis and blame their predicament on a family member or on someone or something outside the family. In so doing, family members may not accept responsibility for contributing to the crisis. Such blaming may overburden the family member who is blamed.

Blaming oversimplifies the problem, keeping families from clarifying and understanding their situation. Oversimplification of what is often a complex problem keeps families from exploring the various options available in order to cope effectively. Reality is thus distorted as family members fail to accept responsibility for either the cause or the solution to the problem.

Family crises are not always as simple as an outside event bringing about a tragedy. Family crises may originate from within, as in the case of adolescent drug use. When this occurs, it might be easy for the parents to blame their teenager for the family crisis. On the other hand, one contributing factor of drug use might be an unstable family situation. Placing blame on either the adolescent or the unstable home life prevents the adolescent or the family from seeing the complexity of the crisis.

As long as the adolescent blames his situation on his parents, personal responsibility is avoided and a solution will not be found. In the same manner, as long as a family focuses only on the drug problem, attention is diverted away from other difficulties. One study of families with adolescent drug dependency found that parents sometimes used blame as an excuse to avoid their own problems, such as difficulty in the marriage. In this same situation, the acting out teenager functioned as a stress absorber within the family, often regressing in order to shift the focus toward himself and away from his parents and their relationship.

Blaming enables the blamer to avoid responsibility while adding to the devaluation of the one being blamed. Additionally, blaming may provoke conflict between family members. To say the least, when this coping mechanism is used, it becomes counterproductive to a family's growth through a crisis.

Cut Off

Some people deal with demands from family members by cutting off the relationship or distancing themselves from others. These people withdraw, either emotionally or physically, from the situation that causes the tension.

An obvious example of cutoff is divorce. A not so obvious example occurs when the couple chooses to remain together, but one or both tunes out of conversations, choosing instead to remain emotionally distant. Such distance in a relationship can magnify an existing crisis or even bring about a crisis.

Capitalizing on Each Other's Strengths

The beginning point in capitalizing on each other's strengths is identifying the uniqueness of each family member. Simply recognizing how each person in the family responds during a crisis is a step toward capitalizing on family members' unique abilities.

It naturally follows that the next step is respecting family members' unique abilities and strengths. We do this by not demanding that others conform to our way of thinking or responding. Respecting family differences allows the family to draw strength from each other.

My family grew in our ability to identify and respect each other's uniqueness, particularly during our daughters' teenage years. An example relates to the talkativeness of family members. Our oldest daughter, Tanya, is quite verbal, while Allison, our youngest daughter, is more introspective. While this is not always the case since they have become adults, it was true during their teen years. I must admit that Tanya took on characteristics of my personality, and Allison took on characteristics of her mother's personality. It is natural for Tanya or me to introduce a particular subject for a family discussion. If something happens, whether good or bad, we want to talk about it. Connie and Allison, on the other hand, might be more reluctant to bring up a situation for discussion, choosing instead to process it internally.

During those years, we learned to value the differences in each other's personalities. Tanya and I learned the value of thinking before talking, and Connie and Allison learned the value of being more open to discuss their feelings. When we try to push the other person to respond like ourselves, the potential for conflict grows. We learn that our family can draw strength from each family member's uniqueness. This approach has been particularly helpful during times of crisis. We continue to learn that it really is okay to be different.

Personal Learning Activity

1. List a strength of each member of your family.

_____

_____

_____

_____

2. List ways your family could capitalize on these strengths during a crisis.

_____

_____

_____

_____

_____

SUMMARY

Our goal in this chapter has been to look more objectively at our families and the way family members relate to one another. In order to move toward this goal, we began by clarifying our assumptions about families: families are more than the sum of individual family members; families have unique patterns of relating; some ways families relate are constructive while others are destructive. We then looked at five characteristic ways most families relate. Though these ways are often unconscious, most families (1) move toward balance, (2) develop rules, (3) develop structures of authority, (4) develop triangles, and (5) develop a particular closeness/distance barometer.

We followed with a listing and discussion of the effects of a crisis on families. Families in crisis (1) experience change, (2) experience disruption of their routine, (3) feel out of control, (4) have disturbing emotions triggered, (5) find their communication patterns altered, and (6) experience time pressure and increased fatigue. The chapter concluded with a look at how families can capitalize on family differences.

In the next chapter, we will look at how families use a crisis as an opportunity for growth. We will see how families who function well prior to a crisis are able to withstand a crisis and even grow in the process.

NOTES

1. The three points covered below are taken from Jerry M. Lewis, *How's Your Family?* (New York: Brunner/Mayel, 1979) 42–44.

2. Ronald Richardson, *Family Ties That Bind* (Seattle: Self-Counsel Press, 1987) 9.

3. Ibid., 12–13.

4. Ibid.

5. Swindoll, *Growing Wise in Family Life* (Portland OR: Multinomah Press, 1988) 152.

6. Richardson, *Family Ties*, 51–68.

Chapter 4

FAMILIES USING A CRISIS AS AN OPPORTUNITY FOR GROWTH

May you be made strong with all the strength that comes from his glorious power, and may you be prepared to endure everything with patience, while joyfully giving thanks to the Father, who has enabled you to share in the inheritance of the saints in the light. (Col 1:11-12, NRSV)

Uncle Harry and Aunt Beth Lepper are role models for me in the way they have responded to crises. Having experienced a variety of misfortunes during their forty years of marriage, no crisis hit them quite like the discovery that Uncle Harry had cancer.

Before I describe that crisis, let me tell you a little about their background. Through the years, Harry has been a farmer, butcher, then poultry producer. In addition to being a homemaker, Beth has had several secretarial jobs. One of these was at the Advent Christian Village in Dowling Park, Florida, which (at the time) consisted of a retirement village, nursing home, and children's home. Several years ago, with their three children grown, they began to sense God's call to minister in the children's home as house parents. After discussing this possibility with the appropriate person and being approved by the administration, they became house parents in this Christian children's home.

The length of their tenure as house parents is an indication of their health as a family and also their sense of calling to care for children from troubled backgrounds. With the average stay of house parents (in the state of Florida) at about eighteen months, Uncle Harry and Aunt Beth completed nine years (at the writing of the first edition of this book). As you might have guessed by now, Harry and Beth are devout Christians.

Only a year after they started as house parents, and when the pain in his shoulder didn't seem to go away, Harry went to the doctor for an examination. Test revealed the presence of multiple myeloma, a type of cancer affecting the bone marrow. Their response to this news was typical of those who learn of a malignancy. Feelings ran the gamut from disbelief to denial and anger. While Harry responded with confidence that God would see them through, Beth responded with disbelief and questioning.

Beth has no qualms about relating her feelings. "If ever I questioned the Lord, I did then," she said. Harry was hospitalized about thirty miles away, and Beth traveled to see him daily. She reported struggling emotionally and spiritually for the first three weeks. Then, one morning as she prepared to visit Uncle Harry in the hospital, she resolved the matter, making sense of what seemed senseless. She was able to say with her lips and finally believe in her heart, "We're going to live every day to the fullest! We're not going to quit! The Lord is going to be with us, and, come what may, He will see us through!" She said there have been bad days since that day, but God has indeed been with them as individuals and as a family.

Many questions flooded their minds in the days following the discovery. How long would he live? What treatment was available? Was there hope of a cure or at least of arresting the spread of cancer? How could this happen to them? They had felt a deep sense of calling to become house parents only a year before, and now one of them had cancer. How could they carry on as house parents, and, if that job were physically possible, would the children's home allow them to continue?

They faced their feelings openly with their biological children as well as with their foster children. With the support of friends and family and with the encouragement of the children's home director, they continued to serve as house parents. Though this was difficult for their tightly knit community and particularly difficult for the foster children, it was felt that the children should not be shielded from this adversity. Dr. Bradley, director of the children's home, reminded my aunt and uncle that heartaches come to all families. He felt that if they resigned as house parents, they would send the wrong signal to the foster children. So they agreed to stay, giving the message to the children that family members in crisis do not abandon the rest of the family; families stick together in good times and in bad times. All of the foster children had experienced trauma within their biological families, so crisis was not new to them. What was new was to be part of a family that responded to crisis in a healthy way.

Since his cancer was discovered, Harry has undergone literally hundreds of trips to the hospital for treatment, several extended periods of hospitalization, and surgery on two occasions. Once a strong and stately man, he now walks with a cane in a stooped condition. On more than one occasion he has been confined to a wheelchair and told he would never walk again. Defying the odds, he not only walks but has also lived well beyond the time expected by medical experts. His optimistic and courageous spirit is due in no small part to his deep and abiding faith as well as the support and prayers of his Christian friends and family. I'm not suggesting that Uncle Harry's and Aunt Beth's response to this crisis has been perfect. I am suggesting that they have made the best of a bad situation. Their stamina and faith during this crisis has inspired everyone who meets them. They have capitalized on the crisis and claimed it as an opportunity for further growth as individuals and as a family.

Recall that the Chinese symbol for crisis suggests that such experiences present us with both danger and opportunity. Crises are dangerous for families. Families become vulnerable to disintegration during a crisis. The potential is present for vulnerabilities to become disabilities. Crisis can lead families to despair.

The other side of the coin presents crisis as an opportunity for growth. Families have the potential of using the difficult situation as the occasion to make them better than they were before. For example, a crisis can function as a clue to family members that something aside from the crisis is wrong. Then the family may benefit from the crisis by doing what is necessary to grow as a family. This occurs when a crisis causes families to secure professional help to see them through the crisis and also to help bring about long-term growth.

Whether or not professional help is sought, a family crisis can give family members an opportunity to draw closer together and strengthen their relationships. Sometimes our fast pace prevents us from making time for important conversations with family members. A crisis can cause family members to slow down enough to spend larger amounts of quality time together.

One young woman described the months prior to her mother's death as a significant period in the life of her family. Hours and days were spent in the hospital as her mother underwent treatment. These times became occasions for meaningful conversations. Reflecting on those days, this young woman said, "It wasn't fun sitting with Mother as she declined and eventually died. I'll always remember the opportunity it afforded us, however, to grow closer together and have conversations we might not have had if it had not been for her illness."

Just as exercise benefits our physical bodies, a crisis can benefit families. Exercise places stress on our muscles and strengthens them. Too much stress on our muscles causes collapse. Just the right amount makes us stronger.

Similarly, crisis can cause families to become stronger. But, like too much exercise, an overwhelming crisis can cause our families to collapse.

Crisis can lead in the direction of danger or opportunity. Disintegration is possible, but so is growth. What, then, keeps a crisis from overwhelming a family? One significant factor that contributes to a family's ability to grow through a crisis is a family's health before the crisis occurred. While few families would claim perfect health, the relative status of the family's health contributes to coping power. Studies have shown that poor family functioning before a crisis predisposes the family to adjustment problems after a crisis.[1] On the other hand, families that function well prior to a crisis are more likely to consider the crisis as a challenge.

Some family scholars use the terms "functional" and "dysfunctional" to describe the relative health of families. In her book, *Stress and the Healthy Family*, Delores Curran explains these two categories and the manner in which families face crisis: "The functional family is one who, when faced with a stress [a crisis is an extreme stress], draws upon its resources to meet that stress and often becomes a stronger family as a result of conquering it. A dysfunctional family is unable to discover enough resources to cope with the stress and as a result allows the stress to further strain or even fragment the family."[2]

What are some characteristically healthy and unhealthy responses families can have when crisis comes home? We will take a brief look at unhealthy responses and a more thorough look at healthy responses.

UNHEALTHY WAYS FAMILIES DEAL WITH CRISIS

Families in crisis sometimes use unhealthy or counterproductive coping mechanisms. These ways of coping temporarily relieve the stress but usually have the long-term effect of adding to a family's crisis. Examples of unhealthy ways of coping (discussed in chapter 3) are blame, prohibition against sharing feelings, denial, poor communication, and rigidity.

Physical violence and substance abuse (considered in chapter 1), can also be contributing factors in other forms of crisis. These forms of behavior may be one way families try to cope with stressful situations. Obviously, neither physical violence nor substance abuse is compatible with family health and growth. The presence of either indicates dysfunction and offers families a clue that they need professional help. When these exist along with an additional crisis, the family's well-being is severely jeopardized.

HEALTHY WAYS FAMILIES DEAL WITH CRISIS

What determines whether or not a family is healthy? How do we determine that one family is healthy and another family is sick? Dr. Jerry M. Lewis offers a simple but profound definition of a healthy family: "A healthy family is one that does two things well: preserves the sanity and encourages the growth of the parents and produces healthy children."[3] There are certainly more comprehensive definitions, but this seems on target.

For our purposes, we are considering how healthy families respond to crisis. Several studies point to the positive and helpful ways families deal with crisis. I draw heavily on the primary research of these studies in providing a list of healthy ways families can deal with crisis.[4]

Identifying the Stressor but Focusing on the Positive

A beginning point for families to cope effectively with a crisis is to identify the stressor but focus on the positive. At first glance, it may seem that identifying the stressor causes the family to focus on the negative. Indeed, it is important for families to focus on the negative stressor long enough to assess their situation. This needs to occur so that families can begin to resolve their problem or situation. However, there is a fundamental difference in focusing on the negative in order to make an assessment and dwelling only on the negative. Dwelling on the negative may cause a family to become stuck. Focusing on the stressor long enough to assess the situation helps a family resolve the crisis so that they can move toward positive strategies of coping.

It's not always easy for families to assess the cause and cure of a crisis. Families seldom deal with a single stressor. Multiple changes and demands seem to happen at once. Consider the variety of crises mentioned in chapter 1. If a family experienced only one of these at a time, they might find it easy to cope, but it's seldom that simple. As often as not, a family experiences more than one crisis simultaneously. For example, a child may be entering first grade (a developmental crisis). At the same time, his mother is hospitalized (an acute crisis). One crisis alone brings stress to a family, but as crises pile up, additional strain and hardship affect the family's time and financial resources. The father may have to adjust his schedule so that he can care for children while also working extra hours in order to pay for additional financial obligations. Efforts at coping may resolve part of the crisis but cause tension in another area.

As mentioned in chapter 1, naming the crisis is a beginning. Having accomplished this task, family members need to be encouraged to focus on the positive. One family chose to direct their attention on the positive by taking time at each meal to mention something for which they were thankful. During this time, their six-year-old son told how happy he was that Daddy could be with them more now than before. This had a positive impact on the mother, who was focusing only on the negative side that her husband was with them more now because of an extended illness. The child's expression of gratitude helped her feel better about the illness and take advantage of the father's presence.[5]

"Reframing" is a word used to describe what happens when a person in crisis sees the positive. One man who was an educator for twenty years lost his job and became ill at about the same time. He reframed his situation and came to see that it was time to accept the challenge and move on to something else. We can view a crisis as either a problem or a challenge. Reframing the situation, seeing it as a challenge instead of a problem, enables families to cope more effectively.

Another approach that accentuates the positive is called self-talk. Self-talk has been used effectively with depressed individuals. This is one tool that is part of a broader treatment area known as cognitive therapy. Cognitive therapists focus on thought processes and have found that people sometimes prolong their discomfort by negative self-talk, constantly dwelling on the bad aspects of their situation and thinking about their desperate situation. The goal of cognitive therapy is to help people think positive thoughts and leave the negative cycle. How you feel is affected by what you tell yourself about yourself. This does not mean ignoring reality but rather choosing, whenever possible, to focus on the positive aspects of the situation. By doing so, we can lower our level of stress and pursue more positive action.[6]

I use this approach when working with people in counseling situations. I draw a circle with the word "event" at the top, then I write several phrases around the circle: "I think," "I feel," "I need," and "I act or I do." I explain that when an event happens, we have immediate thoughts. Our thoughts, or interpretation of the event, arise from our experiences and what my friend Dr. Wade Rowatt calls "the dictionary in our heads." If we are depressed, we often distort the situation negatively. Sometimes we move around the circle, bypassing what we think, feel, and need and going directly to action. More precisely, we react. I suggest that it's better to slow down the process and reflect on each aspect of this awareness circle. What are my thoughts? Am I distorting negatively?[7]

Families can use reframing and positive self-talk to lower anxiety about a crisis. Just as a painting takes on new dimensions as it is framed differently, so too a family crisis can take on different characteristics when seen in a positive light. Families are better able to cope effectively with a crisis and grow through the crisis when they identify the stressor but focus on the positive.

After asking ourselves what we think about a given situation, it's good to reflect on our feelings. What do I feel? I have found that men often have difficulty describing and owning their feelings. I have heard men say "I feel" about a given situation, but the words that follow describe thoughts rather than feelings. I remember working with a declining church. I worked with small groups and one of my questions was, "How do you feel about the situation in your church?" One woman said, "I'm sad." Another woman said, "I'm mad." A man said, "I think we just need to move on." The women accurately described feelings. The man's response, while not describing feelings, betrayed his feelings of fear about discussing the situation.

Having reflected on your thoughts and feelings regarding a specific event, ask, "What are my needs?" Sometimes this may seem like a fruitless process. We may need the situation to change, and the situation may be unchangeable. Sometimes we may be so focused on the needs of others that we have difficulty even thinking about our own needs. On the other hand, we may be so focused on our needs that we fail to see the needs of others. Someone has suggested that the most narcissistic person in the world is someone who is sick. We can be so focused on our pain that we fail to see beyond ourselves. So, in a family crisis, it is good to reflect on the needs of each family member. Sometimes the crisis causes us to focus on the needs of one family member to the exclusion of others. Families need to ask, "What are my personal needs and what are the needs of each family member?"

Knowing what family members think, feel, and need can inform our actions. Points on this awareness circle are reminders that each area of our awareness is important in deciding how to act. If you are blind to your feelings, your judgment may be impaired. If your thinking or interpretation of an event is distorted or, to put it another way, if you "fudge negative" regarding your interpretation of an event, then your feelings and actions are affected. You may not have direct control of your feelings, but you have some control of your thinking. If your thinking (how you frame an event) is positive, your feelings may be more positive.

Having looked at thoughts, feelings, and needs, families can then begin to assess actions. What can each family member do to help the situation?

Personal Learning Activity

1. Think about a stressful time your family experienced that you may or may not have considered a crisis. Complete the following sentence starters.

• Regarding this situation, one thought I have is . . .

_____
_____
_____

• Regarding this situation, one feeling I have is . . .

_____
_____
_____

• Regarding this situation, one need I have is . . .

_____
_____
_____

• Regarding this situation, one thing I can do to help is . . .

_____
_____
_____

2. Now think of positive ways of viewing this situation. What positive self-talk or ways of reframing your situation might have helped? Jot your notes here. Consider discussing this with family members during a meal or another time when all family members are present.

_____
_____
_____
_____
_____

PULLING TOGETHER

Families are better able to face a crisis if they are already accustomed to pulling together as a family. If, on the other hand, family members are not in the habit of sharing responsibilities prior to a crisis, they are at a disadvantage when a crisis occurs. If a family has a constant battle over who does what, a crisis only adds fuel to the conflict. Instead of focusing energy on solving the problem, they needlessly waste emotional strength deciding (or arguing about) which family member will be responsible for which chore or need. A family crisis brings numerous changes and additional burdens that become magnified, particularly for the family that doesn't pull together.

In some families, each member has learned to assume various responsibilities for life together by supporting one another and generally working toward the same goals. Families who practice this kind of behavior prior to a crisis are better able to combine their efforts and face the challenges of a crisis when one arises. Families who are unaccustomed to sharing responsibilities can certainly grow in this regard when a crisis comes home.

Pulling together takes willingness on the part of family members. Each member must *want* to work together; it is difficult to force family members to pitch in and do their part. How then, do families learn to work together, particularly when one family member tends to avoid carrying his or her share of the load?

The ideal would be for each family member to share household and family responsibilities willingly. In this ideal family, husband and wife are flexible in their roles and responsibilities, and children share according to their ages and abilities. Of course, what family lives in an ideal world? What person lives in an ideal family?

In an effort to move toward this ideal, a beginning point might be to have a family discussion about the particular responsibilities of each family member. Family members could be given choices about which chores they will do. One key to helping family members pull together is fairness. Is one family member overloaded, or does each carry his or her fair share? Ages and abilities must be taken into consideration regarding fairness.

Another key to family cooperation is allowing each family member to have input in family decisions. Who wants to be required to cooperate toward achieving a goal when they have no voice in setting the goal? Family members need to decide together the consequences in cases of misconduct or unacceptable behavior. Discussions about accountability in advance help move the family toward cooperation.

Family cohesion equals family strength, whether during normal times or during a crisis. This kind of healthy cohesion is marked by closeness between family members as well as individuals who have the capacity for their own ideas and feelings.

In healthy families, each family member shoulders a portion of the enormous load brought about by adversity. No one person feels totally responsible for the many big and little tasks that must be done. Healthy families are knit together in a relationship based on care for one another and mutual participation in the family enterprise.

Personal Learning Activity

1. Describe how your family pulled together during a difficult period. If your family has not faced a crisis, describe how your family shares daily responsibilities.

_____

_____

_____

_____

_____

2. Write about how your family respects the unique personality of each family member. If this has not been one of your family's strengths, jot notes about how your family can improve in this area. What might each person in the family do to move the family toward the goal of respecting each other?

_____

_____

_____

_____

_____

COMMUNICATING CLEARLY AND OPENLY

Another key ingredient in helping families grow through a crisis is open and clear communication. Families are enabled to pull together with positive and helpful communication patterns. As with other healthy patterns of relating, families who practice open and clear communication prior to a crisis are better able to cope when a crisis arises.

Good communication includes sharing information as well as feelings. Families who communicate find themselves in a better position to solve problems related to a crisis. These families are not exempt from daily frustrations or traumatic experiences. However, families who practice good communication are able to ease daily frustrations and also increase their problem-solving effectiveness from day to day and when faced with a crisis.

Poor communication habits such as criticizing, acting superior, and failing to listen intensify during a crisis. For this reason, inferior communication accentuates instead of minimizes a crisis. Problems become compounded as conflict over decision making adds to an existing crisis.

Communication, whether good or bad, is the process through which we relate to others. Good communication skills translate into good relational skills. Families with good communication and relational skills are not encumbered with unnecessary conflict when crisis occurs. Where good communication is the norm, family members feel like part of the family; they feel as if they belong because they are updated about vital information. They feel an emotional connection. In such families, family members give and receive respect for each other.

Families with healthy communication are characterized by respect for the feelings and opinions of others. This doesn't mean there is always total agreement. It means each family member may voice his or her opinions as everyone strives to make decisions together. Through negotiation or compromise, sometimes families can achieve solutions to what seems like an impasse. At other times, one or both parents must make an arbitrary decision. In healthy families, whatever the decision, the opinions of all family members are heard and valued.

Communication, then, is of utmost importance in the way a family relates. Based on this assumption, how can families increase the effectiveness of their communication and therefore increase their ability to cope with a crisis?

First, turn down the volume. Family conversations that begin in a normal tone of voice sometimes escalate into an uproar. The conflict may occur for a variety of reasons. Putdowns can trigger defensiveness, which can result in shouting matches. Respect and affirmation, on the other hand, beget a more pleasant tone. Most of us know what agitates a particular family member, and we know how to avoid it or present it in a better way. We also know what elicits a more peaceful and sensible response.

A loud volume level doesn't necessarily mean others hear us. On the contrary, loud conversations lead quickly to disrespect for the other person's feelings. This cycle of deteriorating conversation adds a burden to families with a crisis.

Once we turn down the volume, the next step toward healthy communication is to plan to spend time every day talking with family members. The important word here is "plan." Families with dual careers and children and/or teenagers involved in various activities may find little time together.

Time for family conversation is important, but time does not come automatically. We must plan to spend time talking.

My family, though not an ideal model, works at guarding our time to talk. Two important times for us are breakfast and the evening meal. At breakfast we talk about the day ahead, and at the evening meal we talk about the day we've had. Mornings are usually rushed, with each person preparing his or her own breakfast. In spite of this, we parents make an effort to sit down with the children—even though it may be at different times—and discuss the day ahead.

Except for one or two evenings a week when one or more of us must head to a lesson or a practice, evening meals are less hurried. We have guarded this time as a family. With few exceptions, it is a time with the TV turned off. It is usually unstructured time centered around the activities of the day. We celebrate each other's successes and share each other's hurts.

Another way families can improve communication is by learning to express feelings as well as facts. Sometimes facts and feelings are confused. It's usually good to begin with facts, making certain we understand what the other person is saying before we rush to share feelings. When we aren't clear on the information, we may respond with an inappropriate feeling. It's possible to become angry about something when, if we had the facts straight, we might not have become angry at all.

One way to slow down the process of communicating and therefore reduce the possibility of conflict is to confirm what the other person is saying. Asking for clarification is a simple but effective method of being certain we heard the person correctly. Another way to arrive at a clear understanding is to repeat, in our own words, what we hear the other person saying. This allows the first person to confirm or clarify what is meant. Both parties are then able to share the same meaning about the message.

Seeking clarification helps families improve the process of their communication and often decreases or eliminates an uproar. Once families achieve clarification about facts, they can share feelings. These feelings, though sometimes negative, are thus related to what is being communicated and not to some misunderstood message or assumption.

During times of crisis, families benefit from open communication by being able to express feelings freely about their situation. Crises usually bring about strong feelings. When crisis comes home, family members may experience feelings of anger, fear, guilt, uncertainty, anxiety, and loss. The ability to express these feelings is one step in the direction of growing through the crisis.

Families with healthy patterns of communicating practice talking as well as listening. For communication to take place, there must be a sender as well as a receiver. In order for a receiver to understand the message that is sent, he or she must listen.

Keep communication honest, but make it kind. Good communication involves saying what you mean and meaning what you say. Speaking honestly includes telling the truth as well as avoiding manipulative conversation. Family members are guilty of manipulation when they resort to bullying, blaming, or controlling. "They don't play on dependency," said Stinnett and DeFrain. "They aren't silent, long-suffering martyrs to create guilt. All those methods of manipulating others lead to a falseness and shallowness in relationships."[8]

Honesty is no excuse for unkindness. Healthy families maintain a balance between these two extremes. "They aren't apt to let Sis go out in a dress and hairdo that look ridiculous," said Stinnett and DeFrain, "because they don't want to offend her. On the other hand, they won't use one mistake in her judgment as an excuse to blast her taste, time management, hygiene, and study habits."[9]

Personal Learning Activity
List three characteristics of good communication. Choose one positive step your family could take to improve their communication.

_____

_____

_____

_____

_____

GOING WITH THE FLOW

Pine trees grow tall in the soil of Florida, my home state. Seldom do they break, even in the strongest of winds, because they have the unique ability to bend and sway. Their durability comes in part from their flexibility. Another characteristic of the pine tree is its resilience. Even after being blown about by strong winds, the trees keep uprighting themselves; they keep bouncing back.

Strong families need these characteristics of the pine tree. Families are able to withstand the storms of life in part because of their flexibility and resilience. Families need the kind of flexibility and adaptability that allow them to make changes in the wake of a crisis. They need to be resilient enough to bounce back from the crisis.

I'm not talking about adaptability of values. Yes, we live in a changing world and there is a sense in which Christian families need to adapt accordingly. This does not mean we need to compromise our beliefs and values.

A family crisis brings about change that requires families to adapt accordingly. Sometimes events that bring about family disruptions can be changed, but often circumstances are irreversible. In these cases, families must change to respond to events. Crises bring about disorganization and changes in routines. In a crisis, families may feel that their stability is threatened. One response may be to stand firm and remain strong and rigid. Such a response, however, might allow the storm to break families. The ability to flex with the storm helps families survive.

Role flexibility is a primary way in which family members adapt to change. Nowhere is this more evident than with military families during the call-up of active and reserve troops. Today's military service is different than in the past. More women serve, and in some cases both parents serve. Many reservists joined in order to take advantage of the educational benefits. Satisfied and established with their civilian career, they were not prepared for the call to active duty. Whether they come to a reservist or an active duty military person, orders to the battlefield bring family disruption.

The call leaves many suddenly single parents. Role flexibility is of utmost importance for the survival of these military families. The husbands left behind with children often find themselves fulfilling the moms' role of nurturer. Moms find themselves taking care of household repairs, vehicles, and many other tasks that their husbands previously did.

The long-term effect of the current wars in Iraq and Afghanistan on individuals and families will greatly exceed the immediate crisis. For example, one current estimate suggests "a minimum of 300,000 psychiatric casualties from service in Iraq [. . .] with an estimated lifetime cost of treatment of $660 billion. That is more than the actual cost of the war to date [2007]."[10]

Recent estimates say that as many as one out of five of those serving in Iraq or Afghanistan return with posttraumatic stress disorder (PTSD). A study of the first 100,000 veterans returning from Iraq and Afghanistan showed that one out of four had some kind of mental health diagnosis. Of these, more than half had two or more mental health diagnoses. Most common of these problems were PTSD, substance abuse, and depression.[11]

Returning military personnel have the need to resolve these traumas and other emotional issues experienced while deployed. Spouses who were left at home and became accustomed to taking care of day-to-day family responsibilities must make room for the reentry of husbands and fathers (or wives and mothers) to the family. In this sense, reentry of those who have been away brings about a unique set of challenges. Renegotiation of roles becomes the order of the day as families readjust to living in the same house and return to "normal" routines.

The ability to be flexible helps families deal with crises such as these. The ease with which families make such changes affects the amount of conflict in daily interactions. Families who rigidly hold on to role expectations will experience greater disruptions than more flexible families.

Personal Learning Activity

As your family has faced changes, how has your flexibility helped you cope? What advantage do you see in being flexible?

_____

_____

_____

_____

_____

USING RESOURCES WISELY

A family's ability to seek valuable support from others helps them cope with a crisis. Healthy families are able to draw on their own resources and, when needed, draw strength from others. It is a mark of health for a family to recognize the need for outside help and reach out for it. Community service agencies, social services, churches, neighbors, friends, and professionals are often ready and willing to help.

One of the first places many families look for support is the extended family and network of friends. Charlie Warren, former editor of a family magazine, tells an interesting story related to his family's adoption of a special-needs child. Prior to the adoption, a psychiatrist did a family study. In the interview with the Warren couple, the psychiatrist asked them to name the people in their circle of friends who would loan them $25.00. He asked this in order to ascertain the strength of the family's relationship with supportive friends. To the psychiatrist's surprise, Mrs. Warren began naming numerous people who would make such a loan if needed. Families in crisis are strengthened as they are able to draw on the resources of their circle of friends.

Beyond reaching out to those networks of friends and family, a family in crisis may need to assess the availability of professional help. What social services and professional resources are available in your area related to the specific crisis? Many professionals now specialize in particular areas of family need. Families in crisis need to learn about the availability of such professionals. Those who could provide the needed resources for finding such specialists might be a pastor, chaplain, social service agency, family physician, psychologist, pastoral counselor, or other professional.

In addition to professional resources, many worthwhile self-help groups exist to assist families and family members in crisis. Though these are not always tied to the church, many are helpful. Alcoholics Anonymous for alcoholics, Al-Anon for spouses of alcoholics, and Alateen for teenage children of alcoholics have been effective in helping break the cycle of alcoholism. Support groups to meet many other needs have proliferated in recent years. If you are aware of such a group in your area specifically related to your family crisis, please evaluate the group by getting information and a recommendation from a trusted friend or professional.

Additionally, Sunday school classes in some churches and life support groups in others have been a tremendous resource to provide friendship, accountability, and help for families in crisis.

Personal Learning Activity
In thinking about resources available to your family in times of crisis, name three friends you could call to take care of your house or children in the absence of one or both parents.

1. _____
2. _____
3. _____

DRAWING ON SPIRITUAL RESOURCES

Some varieties of pine trees grow tall and withstand strong winds. As suggested already, their strength comes in part because of their flexibility and resilience. They are also able to survive storms because of the depth of their roots. I remember once helping my dad dig up a pine stump. After digging a ditch around the stump and cutting the small roots, I thought the stump was ready to be pushed over. I discovered that pine trees have a taproot that goes deep into the soil. Their ability to grow tall and withstand many storms is related both to their flexibility and to the depth of the taproot.

In a similar manner, the ability of families to withstand storms of life is directly related both to their flexibility and to their spiritual depth. We will look more closely at specific spiritual resources in chapter 5; however, know that spiritual resources are of utmost importance in helping families use a crisis as an opportunity for growth.

I say this because I have experienced it. Since a nonbeliever may not interpret this statement as objective, let me add objectivity from a study conducted by Nick Stinnett and John DeFrain. These two men led an extensive research project in which they studied more than 3,000 families in all geographic regions of the United States. This University of Nebraska-based study suggests that one of the six secrets of strong families is spiritual wellness.[12]

This research project did not espouse a particular doctrine. Nevertheless, the evidence clearly shows the importance of spiritual convictions in strong families. It also shows that strong families draw on spiritual resources in times of crisis and thus are able to use a crisis as a growth opportunity.

Personal Learning Activity

Have you experienced the value of spiritual resources during a family crisis? If so, write a couple of sentences that help you recall how you were strengthened.

_____

_____

_____

_____

_____

_____

_____

_____

SUMMARY

In this chapter we have discussed healthy and unhealthy ways families can face a crisis. A healthy response enables the family to use the crisis as an opportunity for growth. An unhealthy response tends to place additional stress on a family. Healthy responses include the ability to identify the stressor but focus on the positive; to pull together; to communicate in a clear and open way; to adapt; to use resources wisely; and to draw on spiritual resources.

In the next chapter, we will look more closely at several specific spiritual resources available to families.

NOTES

1. Charles R. Figley and Hamilton L. McCubbin, *Coping with Catastrophe, vol. 2 of Stress and the Family* (New York: Brunner/Mazel, 1983) 131, 137.

2. Delores Curran, *Stress and the Healthy Family* (San Francisco: Harper and Row, 1987) 3.

3. Jerry M. Lewis, *How's Your Family?* (New York: Brunner/Mazel, 1979) 4.

4. Research includes Figley and McCubbin, *Coping with Catastrophe*; Curran, *Stress and the Healthy Family*; Lewis, *How's Your Family?*; Nick Stinnett and John DeFrain, *Secrets of Strong Families* (New York: Berkley, 1986).

5. Stinnett and DeFrain, *Secrets of Strong Families*, 125.

6. Bill and Deana Blackburn, *Stress Points in Marriage* (Waco: Word Books, 1986) 45–46.

7. David Burns, in his book, *Feeling Good: The New Mood Therapy* (New York: Avon Books, 1999), suggests that there are ten ways we distort negatively.

8. Stinnett and DeFrain, *Secrets of Strong Families*, 74.

9. Ibid., 20.

10. Evan Kanter, MD, PhD, staff psychiatrist, PTSD Outpatient Clinic of the VA Puget Sound Health Care System, in Bob Roehr, "High Rate of PTSD in Returning Iraq War Veterans," *Medscape Medical News*, 5 November 2007, http://www.medscape.com/viewarticle/565407.

11. Ibid.

12. Stinnett and DeFrain, *Secrets of Strong Families*, 74.

Chapter 5

FAMILIES DRAWING ON
SPIRITUAL RESOURCES

Recalling your tears, I long to see you so that I may be filled with joy. I am reminded of your sincere faith, a faith that lived first in your grandmother Lois and your mother Eunice and now, I am sure, lives in you. (2 Tim 1:4-5, NRSV)

But those who wait for the Lord shall renew their strength, they shall mount up with wings like eagles, they shall run and not be weary, they shall walk and not faint. (Isa 40:31, NRSV)

Strength comes to those who wait, says the prophet Isaiah. We have a problem with this idea, however, because waiting is not in vogue in today's world of instant everything. Our norm is to expect great things *right now.* We are a society accustomed to instant gratification, the instant cure. But when crisis comes home, an immediate remedy is impossible, even in our high-tech world. Concerning the deeper issues of life, such as moving beyond a crisis, the prophet's suggestion to wait becomes effective, even for the modern family. Those who wait on God shall find renewal of strength for family living.

If we could learn to wait, a miraculous transformation would occur. Even God needs room to work on our behalf. Our haste to find a quick answer sometimes prohibits God's ability to exercise power in our lives. The Hebrew word in the Isaiah passage translated "renew" actually means to exchange.[1] The truth of this passage acquires even greater significance when we realize *God* makes the exchange. God takes away our weakness, replacing it with strength. The mysterious exchange does not occur instantly, however. It comes to those who wait on the Lord; it comes to those who wait and yearn for the evidence of God's strength.

Slowly but surely, our weakness is substituted with God's strength. We cannot avoid the crises of life. We must face them squarely. But as we face them, we are called to wait. Waiting sounds passive, but waiting for God is anything but passive. Instead, we wait by doing all that is humanly possible to get help for family members or others in need. Our active waiting may involve nights and days of agonizing prayer to God in concert with loving care for a family member. We actively wait as we identify the source of family pain, focus on the positive, pay attention to the hurts of family members, pull together as a family, and adapt to changes. We actively wait by finding a trusted minister or counselor to whom we can confess our deepest hurts and begin to sort through our feelings. Sharing the burden of our fear, uncertainty, and doubt can activate deeper coping behaviors. God graciously gives our families love and compassion, sometimes working through health professionals.

As we wait, God works for our good, transforming us and transforming adverse circumstances. An exchange of energy takes place, much like a kidney patient receiving dialysis. The old, toxic blood is taken out, and the patient is given new blood. Our energy is renewed as we receive a portion of God's strength.

According to Isaiah, those who wait on the Lord sometimes experience God's strength as ecstasy; they soar like eagles. Other times God's strength is experienced as energy to accomplish important tasks. Occasions exist when ecstasy is inappropriate and when energy to accomplish important tasks seems unavailable. During these times, God's power comes to us in the form of strength to walk and not faint. In whatever manner strength is received, spiritual resources are of utmost importance to families encountering crisis.

Secular researchers term this "spiritual wellness"; regardless of its name, this resource is essential for strong and healthy families. Let's consider the variety of ways Christian families draw strength from spiritual resources.

FAMILIES EXERCISING FAITH IN GOD

Religion is as much a family matter as it is a church matter. In the Old Testament, parents were instructed to teach their children their beliefs in a Holy God. In quoting Deuteronomy 6:4-5, Jesus places this first among the commandments: "'Hear, O Israel: The LORD is our God, the LORD alone. You shall love the LORD your God with all your heart, and with all your soul, and with all your might" (NRSV). The command in Deuteronomy that follows these words places the responsibility of religious training in the home: "Recite them to your children and talk about them when you are at home and when you are away, when you lie down and when you rise. . . . and write them on the doorposts of your house and on your gates" (Deut 6:7, 9,

NRSV). These verses remind us that the family is the environment within which religious faith is nurtured.

This did not change in New Testament times. In his second letter to Timothy, Paul's memory of Timothy's tears also brings to his mind the family who nurtured Timothy in the faith. Though not explicit in his description, Paul says enough to let us know that grandmother Lois and mother Eunice nurtured Timothy in the faith. In these brief words, Paul lifts high the importance of home as a place that hands down the faith.

Though I have not done an objective study, I have observed that families who nurture faith in their members are better prepared to face a crisis. As a pastor for almost fifteen years, I ministered to scores of families in times of grief. In every case, people experienced sadness over their loss. However, families who possessed strong faith, evident in their daily actions, seemed to have a source of strength with which to face the loss. A pastoral counselor friend who works regularly with patients recovering from heart attack and bypass surgery confirms that those with a clear spiritual stance cope much better with their finitude.

On more than one occasion, I have been asked to conduct a memorial funeral service for a person who was not a Christian and whose family members were not Christian. I observed something in these families that I cannot totally describe, but that I will call bewilderment. Their lack of an ongoing relationship with God seemed to leave them bewildered in their grief experience. Even though families and individuals with a strong faith were just as sorrowful, they seemed to possess a certain aura of confidence unknown to non-Christians.

These experiences remind me of the truth of Paul's words in 1 Thessalonians 4:13b: ". . . that you may not grieve as others do who have no hope" (NRSV). Paul seems to assume that even Christians grieve when they lose loved ones. His claim is that those who know the Lord do not grieve in the same way as those without faith.

Christians are also enabled through their faith to possess hope for this life and the next. We are able to claim family hardships as family victories and say with Paul, "And it is no longer I who live, but it is Christ who lives in me. And the life I now live in the flesh I live by faith in the Son of God, who loved me and gave himself for me" (Gal 2:20, NRSV). We are able to sing and live the words of the old song, "Faith Is the Victory."

Families who put their faith into practice prior to a crisis have that faith tested in times of distress. They may feel as though God has abandoned them, but they are enabled to see God's power at work, even in the tough times. Families who are growing in their faith are better able to cope with crisis.

MARKS OF SPIRITUAL WELLNESS

What differentiates spiritual wellness from spiritual illness? Is it active church involvement or some other visible sign? Spiritual wellness ought to manifest itself in outward display; however, a family actively involved in the life of the church is not necessarily spiritually healthy. Physical abuse, emotional abuse, and other dysfunctional behaviors have been observed within families who are actively involved in church attendance. Even when such extreme forms of dysfunction are not present, what appears to be spiritual health may be superficial. In such cases, religious practices may be an outward show and have no positive bearing on the way a family relates.

Spiritual wholeness has to do with how well a family practices faith within the home. It includes relationships within the home and outside the home. "Living righteously in a family is a spiritual discipline," says Diana S. Richmond Garland, dean of the Baylor School of Social Work at Baylor University. Garland further holds that within the context and intimacy of the home, families have an opportunity and responsibility to demonstrate and nurture the fruit of the Spirit.

The home where the fruit of the Spirit is practiced daily is the home of a strong family with the strength to face traumatic experiences. While not specifically talking about families, Paul lists the elements of the fruit of the Spirit in Galatians 5:22-23 (RSV): love, joy, peace, patience, kindness, goodness, faithfulness, gentleness, and self-control. The fruit contains ideals for Christians to practice in all relationships. Since family relationships are primary, we keep faith with Paul's intention in these verses if we apply them to family relationships.

The presence of the fruit of the Spirit in families assumes family members know Christ as Savior and Lord. The fruit of the Spirit is a visible sign or an outward expression of an inner relationship with the Living Lord. Paul probably didn't intend this to be a complete list of all the ways in which the indwelling Christ finds expression in individuals or families. Nevertheless, the list becomes instructive for us as we apply it to family living. Let us look at each one as a mark of a family's spiritual wholeness and evidence of a family's well-being. They are also qualities that enable families better to cope with crisis.

Love

Love heads the list, and not by accident. Paul says a few verses earlier (Gal 5:14) that love for neighbor summarizes the whole law. Paul's highest description of love is found in 1 Corinthians 13. The highest personification of love is found in the life of Jesus Christ.

Love is more than sentimental feelings. Love is unselfish caring for another. As Jesus said, "No one has greater love than this, to lay down one's life for one's friends" (John 15:13, NRSV). Families practice this expression of the fruit when they give themselves unselfishly to each other on a daily basis. Love in action becomes the primary mark of spiritual well-being that colors all areas of a family's interactions.

Joy

The word used for joy comes from the same root word for grace. Joy is not necessarily related to the mood of happiness. Joy is more closely identified as one of God's gracious gifts to those who follow Him. The early disciples were said to possess and share joy in spite of persecutions (Acts 8:8; 13:52; 15:3).

Joy is more than superficial celebration; it is more than emotional ecstasy generated by excitement over circumstances. Paul claimed joy both in his afflictions and in times of happiness. Christian joy is God's gracious gift to families in spite of their circumstances. Christian families celebrate joy-fully the gift of Christ and his presence. As we celebrate this gift, the Holy Spirit creates deep joy within us. Our joy permeates all facets of our lives, giving us strength and energy. One mark of family spiritual well-being is the presence of joy.

Peace

The Greek word for peace means harmony. Jewish people used the Hebrew word for peace, *shalom*, as a greeting. Shalom has to do with total well-being. Both the Hebrew and Greek meanings can be applied to Paul's use of the word "peace." Paul uses the word in his letters as a salutation. Paul wishes harmony and well-being for his readers.

Peace includes a right relationship with God, with self, and with others. Families who possess this element are characterized by harmonious relation-ships. Peace is more than an absence of strife, though. It is a gift of God that includes the presence of serenity even amid suffering. Paul suggests that an absence of anxiety is possible with the presence of God's peace: "And the peace of God, which surpasses all understanding, will guard your hearts and your minds in Christ Jesus" (Phil 4:7, NRSV).

Patience

Patience is used in contrast to outbursts of rage discussed in the previous passage of Scripture. Translated "longsuffering" in the King James Version, it is often used in the New Testament to describe God's attitude toward people (see Rom 2:4; 9:22). God in Jesus Christ typifies longsuffering. He is patient with us when we stray or when we exhibit apathy.

One of the great needs of families, particularly during times of difficulty, is patience. A crisis often causes tempers to flare and feelings to surface. The kind of patience Paul writes about is what one person has called "patience with a purpose."[2] God is the source of this kind of patience. Families need to make a conscious effort to practice patience, one of the marks of spiritual well-being.

Kindness

As with the other elements of the fruit of the Spirit, God is the source and Christ is the ideal of kindness. Paul uses this word in conjunction with patience to describe love: "Love is patient; love is kind . . ." (1 Cor 13:4, NRSV). Gentleness is the King James translation. Both translations suggest mildness in relating to others.

Kindness brings together our inner character and outward expression. How different the atmosphere in our families would be if we related with kindness and gentleness. But how often do we forget to practice common courtesy toward family members?

Goodness

The word "goodness" occurs only a few times in the New Testament. One aspect of its meaning relates to values. This person or family has high moral values, modeled after the life and teachings of Jesus Christ. "Goodness" is also used in a general sense to mean that Christians are to be good with a purpose, or good for something. Goodness shows strength as well as sweetness. Like kindness, goodness is a common courtesy expressed in family relationships. It is a mark of family wellness.

Faithfulness

In its context, this word refers to a quality of trustworthiness and fidelity. It has to do with a person's relationship to God that also finds expression in relationship with others. Families need to trust each other and be trustworthy. Married couples need to practice fidelity to their marriage covenant. At a minimum, this means married couples should refrain from sexual relations with another individual.

Faithfulness also applies in other realms. Family members should be trustworthy in their word and deed. This means telling the truth and keeping promises. Faithfulness or trustworthiness is another mark of family well-being.

Gentleness

The King James Version translates this word "meekness." The word "gentleness" is better because meekness has evolved to mean something the original word didn't mean. When you think of a meek person, you probably think of an overly kind, shy, and frail person. This person has what some call a "doormat personality" because people can walk all over him or her.

The word translated "meekness" or "gentleness" in this passage means something else entirely. In the first century, the word was used for an animal tamed and brought under the control of its master. Those who possess this fruit of the Spirit are under the control of their Master, Jesus Christ. They are now gentle, but their strength has not diminished. Instead, their strength is controlled. Not only that, but their strength is supplemented by the strength of God. Families characterized by meekness or gentleness are not weak; rather, they have made Jesus the Lord of their homes. These families and the individuals in them have a gentle strength. Gentleness is another mark of a family's spiritual wellness.

Self-control

The King James Version translates this word "temperance." Paul preached a freedom that did not give free rein to one's impulses and desires. Self-control or temperance may refer to sexual desire, drunkenness, and other "works of the flesh" Paul lists in Galatians 5:19-21. Self-control describes a person who, through Christ's power within, refuses to be swept along by errant desires.

Paul ends his list by saying there is no law against the fruit of the Spirit. Nor is there a law that forces these elements upon families or individuals. However, families who live out these elements are spiritually mature. They live and breathe their commitment to Christ in their daily interaction with one another. They have a reservoir of strength available to them that helps them cope with and grow through a crisis.

Personal Learning Activity

List the nine elements of the fruit of the Spirit Paul spoke of in Galatians 5:22-23. Jot a note beside four of these indicating how each applies to spiritual wellness in the family.

1. _____

2. _____

3. _____

4. _____

5. _____

6. _____

7. _____

8. _____

9. _____

FAMILIES NURTURING FAITH

Having considered key ingredients of spiritual wellness, we see that families who practice their faith in God are better enabled to face crisis. But this kind of faith does not simply happen. There is a sense in which the fruit of the Spirit is beyond our ability to create and control. Just as it is impossible for us to create an apple or an orange, we cannot create the fruit of the Spirit. We can grow fruit, but only God can create fruit. By the same token, only God can create the fruit of the Spirit. We can, however, create the conditions in our families where the Spirit of God has room to do the work of creating fruit of the Spirit. Let's think of ways, then, that families can cultivate faith in God.

Congruence

That's a fancy word for "practice what you preach." This, of course, is easier said than done. Integrity characterized my parent's lives. They maintained high values and expected their children to do the same. Their lives matched the values they espoused. They were congruent. This gave strength to our home, and their example continues to influence my home today.

Children need role models. In fact, parents cannot fail to provide a role model. The question is whether the role model we provide is a good or poor role model. Parents provide worthy models to follow when their lives are congruent. The faith of parents is not automatically passed to children.

Rather, the faith of the parents, when combined with their worthy example, provides a powerful witness to children as well as those outside the home.

Christians Married to Non-Christians

According to studies, a shared faith is an important characteristic of strong families. What about families where one spouse is a Christian and the other is a non-Christian? This is a complex issue. What should a Christian do when his or her spouse is not a believer? This question is not easily answered because no two situations are exactly the same. However, even with the complexity of such situations, we find informative biblical principles.

Paul addresses the subject in 1 Corinthians 7:8-16 and 2 Corinthians 6:14. In the latter passage, Paul does not favor Christians marrying non-Christians. Paul's encouragement that there be a match regarding belief in Christ is as instructive for couples today as in the first and second centuries. In our twenty-first-century world, couples have enough pulling against their marriage as it is. We recognize that this ideal is not always reached in families.

In 1 Corinthians 7:8-16, Paul deals with situations where one of the marriage partners is a Christian and the other is not. In cases where both are non-Christians and one later becomes a Christian, Paul opposes the dissolution of marriage on grounds that they are now mismatched. He recognizes the fact that the non-Christian spouse may object to the newfound faith and religious practices of the other spouse. The potential for open conflict is present in homes where one of the marriage partners is a Christian and the other is not. While Paul opposes divorce on principle, he does allow for divorce when the faith of one spouse creates conflict and the non-Christian partner desires separation.

A Christian spouse gives a quality of goodness to the home not otherwise present. Paul even suggests that the Christian spouse and parent gives a kind of "holiness" (v. 14) to the children. I understand this to mean that the Christian parent helps create a wholesome, Christlike atmosphere that is beneficial to the spiritual development of the children.

The passage ends with the hope that the Christian spouse will win the non-Christian spouse to faith in Jesus Christ. "Wife, for all you know, you might save your husband. Husband, for all you know, you might save your wife" (1 Cor 7:16, NRSV). The believer is encouraged to remain in the marriage and work to create harmony.

Peace is not always possible, and open conflict and even abuse sometimes occur. This can occur in Christian as well as non-Christian families.

While Paul does not address the issue of abuse, he certainly does not seem to require the Christian to remain in such a dysfunctional and hurtful relationship.

How then can we make application of the biblical text to situations in our world today? The ideal is for both marriage partners to be Christians—and to practice Christian values. But we do not live in an ideal world. In day-to-day relationships, Christian spouses, whether married to another Christian or not, can set Paul's elements of the fruit of the Spirit as goals in the way they relate. The Christian's behavior should be congruent with his or her belief. In other words, the Christian should practice love, joy, peace, patience, kindness, goodness, faithfulness, gentleness, and self-control (Gal 5:22-23).

Superficial Spirituality

A problem for some families is lack of congruence. The family may engage in the outward expressions of their faith; they may practice regular church attendance and appear spiritually mature to those outside the home. But what goes on inside the family circle may differ markedly from what is espoused publicly. This may occur for years with little awareness on the part of outsiders.

What should families do to rectify this situation? Sometimes family members are apprehensive about saying anything to other family members because they fear rejection. They may be reluctant to say anything to people outside the family because of the cultural taboo against telling family matters to outsiders.

Family members should be challenged to bring their behavior in conformity to their beliefs. Where abuse is present, the taboo of family silence should be ignored and the proper social agency informed. Confrontation is not easy and, in fact, may add to a family's conflict. However, confrontation may be necessary for growth to take place. A trusted minister or health professional can provide guidance where severe dysfunction is present.

Church Involvement

The outward expressions of religious faith are an important way families nurture faith. When I was a child, our family attended church regularly. That practice continued into my own family. Church involvement as a family played a vital part in the development of my faith. It also played a vital part in the development of our children's faith. Continued church involvement helps to nourish faith and values for my current family, even as the children left home a number of years ago.

My understanding of the Bible was formed as I studied this inspired book in Sunday school. Beliefs about the church, the Bible, God, and Jesus Christ were nurtured in Sunday school. Committed teachers lovingly helped me understand the meaning of great Scripture passages. Sunday school attendance played a fundamental role in my development as a person. Attendance at preaching and worship also helped me apply biblical truths to my life— from childhood to today.

My first experience of worship took place before I can remember, when I was an infant. Our country church did not have a nursery, so everybody attended the worship services. In those services, I gradually became aware of my sinful nature and my need for a Savior. My response to Jesus Christ as Savior and Lord came in a worship service with my parents present. They helped me understand that this decision was one I must make for myself, but their encouragement created the environment in which my decision was made.

My family always attended both worship services on Sunday as well as the midweek prayer service. Each family member went to his or her own Training Union (later Church Training, then Discipleship Training) class. It was in Training Union that I first stood to give my part of the program. Training Union was the "garden" in which my leadership skills were cultivated. I am grateful for parents who made church attendance something the family did together. Active church involvement became one way my family nurtured our faith.

It is impossible to estimate the lasting consequences of a family's active church involvement. Consider John Mark, writer of the Gospel of Mark. Little is said of him in the New Testament; but one significant verse, Acts 12:12, gives us a glimpse of his home life: "As soon as he realized this, he went to the house of Mary, the mother of John whose other name was Mark, where many had gathered and were praying" (NRSV). Peter had been in jail, and a prayer meeting was held on his behalf at the home of Mary, the mother of John Mark. After Peter's miraculous release, he went to Mary's home. He knew to go there because this was the place where the church regularly met. We do not know John Mark's age—he may have been a teenager or even younger—but because the church met regularly in his home, it obviously had considerable influence on his life. Here was a home noted for its Christian hospitality and faith. Church involvement cultivated faith in this young man who later penned the Gospel of Mark.

Family Devotions

At various times in my life, I've been part of a family that had a time of family devotions. I remember one period during my childhood when we gathered around the fireplace and read the Bible. There were times when we children took part by reading the devotional from a family magazine. I remember during my teenage years my dad reading the Bible and having a prayer every morning at breakfast.

When our children were growing up, our family had difficulty consistently maintaining family devotions in the traditional form. We were more consistent in using teachable moments to communicate the "why" of beliefs and values. Sometimes these were related to the comments or questions raised by the children. At other times, these teachable moments occurred over a school assignment or in reference to a television program.

Meal times were important times for our family. We set the tone of this family time by blessing our food. We often used these moments to discuss important personal and family matters. These were special times in which we communicated our faith through words and actions. Even now, during our "empty nest" years, we continue to follow these patterns.

Laughter

You will not find humor listed in the elements of the fruit of the Spirit. Humor is probably not listed as a spiritual discipline. Why am I including laughter in the chapter about families drawing on spiritual resources? I contend that humor is one of God's delightful gifts to families. While I do not suppose to add it as a fruit of the Spirit or a spiritual discipline, I believe good, wholesome laughter is an effective resource for families.

"God has given you and me the unique gift of humor," says Tal Bonham in his book *Humor: God's Gift*, "and I want us to be good stewards of his gift." Humor is not only God's gift to individuals; it is God's gift to families. Bonham has done extensive research on what he calls "the laughter factor" in life. Regarding humor in the home, he says, "Humor, like charity, begins at home." Concerning humor in the marriage relationship, he says, ". . . it is almost a proven axiom that 'husbands and wives who laugh together stay together.'"[3]

Assuming that humor is God's gift to families, what does it do for families, and how can it be used as a resource for families in crisis? Humor adds spice to life. Laughter brings sunshine to family relationships. Humor refreshes families, keeping life exciting and making dull moments bright.

We must admit that some forms of humor are hurtful and should be avoided. Hurtful humor includes words said in jest that contain a putdown of another person. On occasion, cutting messages are sent to a family member through the use of humor. Humor that is hostile or used to ridicule others obviously does not build family relationships.

I recently helped a couple who experienced family pain due to this form of negative humor. The husband had a terrible childhood and, as a result, began using humor as a coping mechanism at an early age. Through his teenage and adult years, he used humor to calm his anxieties even while putting other people down. His wife and son regularly felt the sting of his humor. Needless to say, humor in this family did not refresh their life together.

I am calling for wholesome, clean, and tasteful humor. This kind of humor does not poke fun at family members but is sensitive to the feelings of others. This kind of humor adds freshness to daily interactions with family members and helps families cope during times of crisis.

Surely every family has a clown. That responsibility is joyously mine, for I find humor in the oddest places. Maybe that's what makes it funny. The funniest things, and the things my family enjoys laughing at the most, seem to be things that happen to me. They like for the joke to be on me, and I don't usually mind.

One of my crazy stunts occurred when our family went to a conference center for a week of spiritual refreshment as well as a wholesome family time. This incident became the occasion for hilarity. I was getting ready to take a shower. The whole family (my wife and two children) was in the living room of the apartment. As I bent to turn the water on, I didn't notice that someone had already redirected it from the tub to the shower. Much to my surprise, I got a head full of water! In a burst of anger, I came running into the living room shouting, "Now, doesn't that just *get* you!" Just as quickly, I realized my hilarious predicament: I didn't have a single thread of clothing on. I left as quickly as I arrived, laughing at myself as easily as I initially shouted at my family! Occasionally, when things get tense or when we have a rough time, my family likes to remember the day Daddy ran shouting into the living room with no clothes.

I wish I could say humorous situations always come so easily from hard feelings. When I saw myself as reflected in the looks on my family members' faces, I laughed. I wonder if that's what it might take for families in a crisis. Being able to view the absurdity of our situation is one way of bringing smiles or laughter. Even in our pain and suffering and crises, we can laugh.

Doctors and other professionals now use humor as an aid to help their patients overcome depression. The late Norman Cousins did an extensive study on this subject. In the 1970s, after being diagnosed with a debilitating disease, he prescribed for himself large doses of laughter. "Ten minutes of solid belly laughter," he said, "would give me two hours of pain free sleep." He overcame the illness and lived for a number of years. He did further concrete research of the effects of humor on illness. The results of his studies are reported in the book *Head First*. In this book, he says, "Of all the gifts bestowed by nature on human beings, hearty laughter must be close to the top."[4] He presents scientific evidence to support his claim that humor is an emotional antidote to stress and illness. He also gives numerous examples of how "humor therapy" is used in the medical community.

We recently found humor during what was otherwise a community-wide crisis. Our area experienced two lengthy electrical power outages within six months. The first occurred when the remnants of Hurricane Ike swept through Kentucky. Winds in excess of 70 mph toppled trees and power lines, leaving hundreds of thousands without power. Many people had significant damage to property. Besides the inconvenience of having no electricity, we lost everything in our refrigerator.

Just a few months later, an ice storm caused even greater damage, and a larger number of people found themselves without power. More than 700,000 people in Kentucky were in the dark, and more than 200,000 in the Louisville area had no power. Many people fled to shelters or hotels, while others remained in their homes. Frigid temperatures, one night dipping to eight degrees, added to the difficulty of this crisis. We could hear the hum as many of our neighbors used backup generators to provide light and heat. We were without power for about five days but were able to stay in our home. Gas logs in a downstairs fireplace provided ample heat, and a gas hot water heater allowed us to bathe. We capitalized on the cold weather and moved our refrigerator items to our deck box. We used candles and LED flashlights to see at night.

The Christmas before, an outdoor catalog retailer sold caps with built in LED lights on the bill. I purchased each member of our family one of these "hat lights." During Christmas week, before the hats became a necessity, the grandchildren enjoyed their visit by wearing the hats in dark rooms or closets.

Now that we had no electricity, we put these hats to good use. We weathered the ice storm power outage in style and with good humor. The "hat lights" became a source of much-needed light, but they also brought a light-hearted spirit to our attitudes.

We went few places in the house at night without our hats shining a light in the direction we faced. The lights allowed us to read and also to find our way into darkened rooms, closets, and cupboards. The principal at the school where my wife is a librarian stayed with us for several nights until power returned to her home. We shared one of the hat lights with her. We particularly enjoyed playing dominos one evening. With an LED light suspended from the light fixture over the table and with each of us wearing hat lights, we forgot about the crisis of the power outage. We were comical with our hats turning first this way and then that way, trying to figure out the color and number of dots on the dominos.

Families in crisis can use humor to lighten their load. The tone of a crisis is seriousness that often adds to the heaviness of the situation. Humor and playfulness is one way of decreasing anxiety or stress within the family. To the extent that a person is able to become what Edwin Friedman calls a "non-anxious presence," anxiety is reduced.[5] This can be compared to a step-down transformer in an electrical system. The use of appropriate humor, then, is one way of reducing the stressfulness of a crisis and thereby lightening its burden.

Look for the absurd in your situation. Laugh with your family. Help each other see the humorous side. If you are not able to find anything funny in your current state of affairs, remember a funny incident from your past. Look for the humor in everyday occurrences. Look for humor in magazines and newspapers. Clip these to share with family members. Humor adds spice and freshness to stale and tasteless situations.

Personal Learning Activity

Observe what makes other members of your family laugh. Clip a cartoon or joke to share with your family. Plan to watch a humorous television program that your family enjoys. Observe events that happen to you or to your family with an eye for the humorous. Use the space below to make notes about implementing one of the above suggestions.

_____

_____

_____

_____

HELP FAMILY MEMBERS CLAIM THE BLESSING

Families today need to recapture the Old Testament practice of conveying the blessing. Whether we call it a blessing or simply affirmation, this practice is a mark of spiritual wellness.

In Old Testament times, parents and grandparents used this practice to pass leadership and property down to their descendants. Several biblical examples describe this custom. Genesis 12:1-4 describes how God blessed Abraham and intended for Abraham to become a blessing to others. Genesis 27:18-29 depicts Isaac blessing his son Jacob. Ephraim and Manasseh, the sons of Joseph, were blessed by their grandfather, Jacob (Gen 48:8-22). Jacob wrestled with the angel of the Lord at the Jabbok River and finally received God's blessing at dawn (Gen 32:22-32). Moses blessed the tribes of Israel and provided specific affirmation and encouragement for each tribe (Deut 33:1).

We find in these passages that people used touch and words of affirmation to convey the blessing. The blessing was important in the life of the person who received it. It meant acceptance, affirmation, and good wishes.

Myron Madden has written two books related to the blessing, *The Power to Bless* and *Blessing: Giving the Gift of Power*. In the latter book, he lists the following characteristics of the blessing:

> Blessing is the gift of power.
> It is the gift of the self to another.
> Blessing is our permission.
> Blessing is permission to be as well as to do.
> Blessing is both material and spiritual.
> Blessing sets free.
> Blessing is making another as important as the self.
> Blessing ties the generations together.

Another concept that goes hand in hand with the idea of blessing is the concept of self-esteem. Self-esteem is a person's assessment of his or her worth. One person has said that self-esteem is the mainspring that slates every child for success or failure as a human being. This is not self-conceit. Conceit is simply a whitewash to cover low self-esteem. True esteem for one's self involves a sense of self-respect, of self-worth based on being God's creation.

The family blessing can become the vehicle through which family members develop healthy self-esteem. It is a family matter, after all. Let's face it:

classmates at school will not help one another cultivate healthy self-esteem. Folks in the neighborhood and friends at work are not committed to helping you develop self-respect. Giving and receiving the blessing and thus developing healthy self-esteem is a family matter. Family members have tremendous power to bless. Parents and grandparents, in particular, hold the key to bestowing the blessing.[7]

Personal Learning Activity

Look up one of the passages discussed at the beginning of this section (Gen 27:18-29; Gen 48:8-22; Gen 32:22-32; Deut 33:1), and answer the following questions.

1. What events surrounded the giving of this blessing?

_____
_____
_____
_____

2. How was the blessing conveyed?

_____
_____
_____
_____

3. What was the significance of receiving the blessing?

_____
_____
_____
_____

WAYS OF GIVING THE BLESSING

One way families can give the blessing is through meaningful touch. When a blessing was conveyed in the Old Testament, it was usually accompanied by a touch. In Scripture, the laying on of hands graphically symbolizes the transferring of the blessing's power. Meaningful touch continues to be a way for family members to bless one another. Today the touch of a father or mother or family member is a powerful way of conveying affirmation.

Studies have shown that our body chemistry changes in a positive way through the positive touch of another individual.

The opposite of meaningful positive touching is physical abuse. Just as positive touching becomes one of the ways of conveying a blessing, abusive touching conveys the opposite. Abuse conveys rejection and enhances the development of low self-esteem, whereas positive touching conveys acceptance and affirmation and enhances the development of healthy self-esteem.

Families who practice positive touching not only help family members develop a positive attitude; they also help their families develop healthy family esteem. Family members are enabled to feel good about themselves and view their family in a positive light.

A second way families can share a blessing is through the spoken word. The saying, "Sticks and stones may break my bones, but words will never hurt me" is wrong. Words can hurt deeply or bless deeply. Words can destroy a friendship and rip apart a home. Abuse does not have to include physical harm. Abusive language can hurt a person's spirit just as deeply as physical abuse can harm the body.

Some language, while not severely abusive, may hurt family relationships if it inflicts harm on the person. Putdowns, for example, contribute to the deterioration of family relationships. In recent years, situation comedies have become popular television fare. They often demonstrate poor ways of relating. Frequent putdowns are followed by laughter. In real life, laughter can follow putdowns, but most often the laughter is at the expense of the other person.

Family members, particularly parents, need to think of ways to share a daily affirming word with their children. Instead of trying to catch your child doing something wrong, try to catch him doing something good and affirm him. This principle is also important in the marriage relationship. Affirming words shared with a spouse enhance the other person's self-worth while at the same time adding to the feelings of family esteem.

A third way families can share a blessing is by picturing the future. God blessed Abraham and pictured a special future for him (Gen 12:1-3). David placed a high value on God's blessing for his house and for his future name (2 Sam 7:29).

Family members share a blessing with one another when they wish the best future for each other. Parents need to use this form of blessing with caution to avoid influencing a child to accomplish the parents' own desires. Affirmation of the child's gifts and how they might fit a particular vocation is one way to bless a child.

When our oldest daughter was fourteen years old, she and I were on our way to one of many lessons. She was beginning to think about what vocation she might like to pursue; the top two on the list that particular week were lawyer and interior designer. I suggested that since she enjoyed being with people, she might feel more fulfilled if she chose a career that included working with people more than working with things.

A few weeks later, she took a vocational preference test at school. When she received the results in the mail, she shared them with me. She pointed out that some of the suggestions were more acceptable to her because they involved working with people more than working with things. She affirmed that need in herself. I smiled inside even as tears came to my eyes, for I recognized that she had received the blessing I had tried to give her that day in the car.

A fourth way families can give the blessing is by giving gifts of special significance. In our affluent society, gifts often substitute for love. Even when this is not the case, the large number of gifts received by the average child probably diminishes their worth.

The kind of gift I'm talking about is a gift of special significance. For example, my father inherited a shotgun from his grandfather. Even when I was a young boy, he told me this particular gun would be mine. It became a special gift that conveyed a blessing.

Not long before Dad's death, I was at his home for a visit. He was beginning to lose his memory and was aware that he might not be able to communicate rationally with us much longer. He was a carpenter but had already gotten rid of most of his tools. He saved three antique planes used for making boards smooth, one for each of his three sons. It was a special moment and a powerful blessing when he gave me this special tool. The value of the tool is minimal; the value of the blessing is extremely high.

Christmas can be a special time of gift giving. The gift I remember most was not a gift that appeared under the tree or a gift I received. The gift was given to Allison, our younger daughter, by her grandmother Saidee Jackson.

We were visiting for Christmas holidays during the time when Mrs. Jackson's health rapidly declined. We all knew she might not live to see another Christmas. In fact, she died six months later. I described in chapter 1 how one evening during our visit, we sat on the couch and looked through family photo albums, reminiscing about childhood and earlier days in the family.

Mrs. Jackson wanted to talk about her legal will, making sure her affairs were in order before she died. As she talked about what she was leaving behind and which child should receive which possession, Connie said, "I'd like for you to give each of my children something special for them to remember you by."

The children, then ages nine and twelve, were included in this conversation, so Mama J began asking them what they might want. They discussed the possibility of receiving something special from the china cabinet. A few minutes later, we gathered around the cabinet full of heirlooms. Tanya chose a beautiful tea set and Allison chose a pitcher. Allison wanted to hold the pitcher, and all of us wanted to hear about the origin of these pieces. As Allison sat enthralled, holding the pitcher, we learned that it had been Mrs. Jackson's mother's wedding gift. Each of us received a powerful blessing that night as a grandparent gave special gifts to her grandchildren.

These are four of many ways for families to give a blessing:

(1) Use words of affirmation.
(2) Offer positive and meaningful touch.
(3) Picture a special future.
(4) Give special gifts.

Use these four to generate your thinking and discover other ways to pass on a blessing.

Personal Learning Activity
Write one positive affirmation you can give each family member.

_____

_____

_____

GO BACK TO THE BLESSING

Returning to a special blessing, either physically or in one's memory, helps a person or family face a crisis. This seems to have occurred in the life of Jesus Christ in the days before he faced the crucifixion.

John 10:40 says, "He went away again across the Jordan to the place where John had been baptizing earlier, and he remained there" (NRSV). Jesus journeyed to this special place after his enemies pursued him. We recall that this place was special for Jesus because John baptized him there. There, the Spirit descended on him in the form of a dove and a voice from heaven said, "You are my Son, the Beloved; with you I am well pleased" (Mark 1:11b, NRSV).

Jesus received his Father's blessing at his baptism. If we focus on Jesus' humanity, it seems that his going back across Jordan was his way of going back to the blessing in his life. Going back to the blessing enabled him later to go back across the Jordan and experience with stalwart strength his arrest, trial, and crucifixion. Jesus was enabled, at least in part, to face his most severe crisis by going back to the blessing.

Families today are better able to face the crises of life when they go back to the blessings in their lives. As leaders in the home, parents particularly need to go back to the time when they felt blessed. Recalling a significant blessing from parents, grandparents, or a significant friend brings power to the present situation.

In a family life revival some time ago, I used this text from John's Gospel and encouraged those in attendance to go back and claim a blessing from a parent or other significant person in their lives. The next evening, a young woman came to me to describe what had happened to her. She had gone home the night before and found her mother's Bible. This was special to her because it became hers as a child following her mother's death. She reported finding a piece of paper where her mother had written a prayer for her. The prayer or special blessing had been there all the time, but the daughter only now discovered it. Going back to discover or rediscover a special blessing provides tremendous power for families facing crisis.

Personal Learning Activity

1. As a family, sit together and try to share a blessing you remember from your earlier years. If you received a special gift, show it to each other and explain its significance.

2. If you are a parent or grandparent, ponder ways to bless the children in your life. List these ways.

_____

_____

_____

_____

_____

_____

SUMMARY

In this chapter, we talked about how families can draw on spiritual resources to face a crisis. Spiritual wellness is an important factor in a family's ability to cope with crisis. The fruit of the Spirit, when present in the home, is a mark of spiritual wholeness.

Families can nurture faith and spiritual wellness as they cultivate the fruit of the Spirit and as they practice faith in the home. One significant way families can nurture spiritual wellness is through giving and receiving the blessing.

In the next chapter we will talk about how the church can help families grow spiritually. We will also talk about how churches can help families in crisis.

NOTES

1. Clifton J. Allen, ed., *Proverbs–Isaiah*, vol. 5 of Broadman Bible Commentary (Nashville: Broadman Press, 1971) 302.

2. George Arthur Buttrick, ed., *Interpreter's Bible*, vol. 10 (Nashville: Abingdon Press, 1953) 568.

3. Tal D. Bonham, *Humor: God's Gift* (Nashville: Broadman, 1988) 14, 169.

4. Norman Cousins, *Head First: The Biology of Hope* (New York: E.P. Dutton, 1989) 126–27.

5. Edwin H. Friedman, *Generation to Generation* (New York: Guilford Press, 1985) 208–209.

6. Myron Madden, *Blessing: Giving the Gift of Power* (Nashville: Broadman, 1988) 19–20.

7. I draw heavily from Gary Smalley and John Trent, *The Blessing* (Nashville: Nelson: 1968).

Chapter 6

ALL GOD'S PEOPLE NEED A FAMILY

And pointing to his disciples, he said, "Here are my mother and my brothers!" (Matt 12:49, NRSV)

In this day of the disintegrating family, more than ever before, all God's people need a family. In the last chapter we talked about how spiritual wellness becomes a tremendous resource for families. Of course, the degree of spiritual wellness differs among families. One family may have few spiritual resources on which to draw in a time of crisis, while another family has numerous resources. In either case, a family's relationship to their local church can play a vital role in helping them deal with and grow through a crisis.

Crisis seems to come home in ever-increasing numbers. For this reason, all God's people need a family. The need for extended family and the system of support it can provide is significant. The need for an extended family of faith is even greater. The church and home have the responsibility and privilege of working together to nurture spiritually and emotionally stable families. The home and the church can accomplish together what neither can achieve on its own.

The church family as a family of faith supplements the emotional and spiritual resources of biological families. This was true for a sixteen-year-old member of a metropolitan church. She was interviewed as part of a church-wide study conducted in order to determine the future course of the church's ministries. The interviewer asked, "How did you come to be a part of this church?" The teenager described how her parents abandoned her and how her grandmother reluctantly took her in. Since the church was a short walk from her grandmother's home, she began attending Wednesday evening activities; before long, she accepted Christ and became active in the total life of the church. Then the interviewer asked, "What does this church mean to you?" The young woman answered exuberantly, "This church means everything to me. It gave me a home when I had no home. It gave me a place when I had no place. It helped me know I'm somebody."[1]

This teenager discovered a family beyond her biological family. When crisis came home to her, the church reached out and made her part of the family of faith. Their ministry with her filled a void and provided her the kind of loving support she needed during her developmental teenage years. All God's people need a family, especially a family of faith.

Jesus redefines the meaning of family in the incident recorded in Matthew 12. One day while performing miracles and speaking to a crowd of people, Jesus' mother and brothers came to get him. Evidently unable to get inside because of the large crowd, they sent a messenger to tell Jesus they were there for him. Jesus asked, "Who is my mother, and who are my brothers?" (Matt 12:48b, NRSV). With this simple, yet profound statement, Jesus forever redefined family.

We do not choose our biological families; however, being a part of God's family is a choice. Those who choose to obey God and follow Jesus Christ become part of this family. The welcome mat is out for all, even those deprived of traditional family relationships.

Many people in first-century Palestine were excluded from both their own families and from a relationship to God's family. Jesus came that they too might have life and be a part of God's family. The Ethiopian eunuch, because of his physical state, is a biblical example of one who was excluded from the people of God (see Deut 23:1). Acts 8:26-40 describes how Philip joined this eunuch in his chariot while the eunuch read the book of Isaiah. After Philip explained the Scriptures to him, this man who had no family became part of God's family through Jesus. "Those who are deprived of traditional family relationships can therefore become members of a greater family," says David Garland. "This family is open to all and especially those who are normally cut off from family relationships."[2] For this reason, Paul urged Philemon to accept the runaway slave, Onesimus, back into his household, not as a slave but as a brother. All people—whether slave or free, male or female, Jew or Gentile—can be part of the family of faith brought into being by Jesus Christ (see Gal 3:28). In our world, this means churches need to be inclusive, reaching people from all socioeconomic and ethnic groups with no regard for their resources to give back to the church.

For one reason or another, many people in our world today feel cut off or isolated from family. The percentage of single adults continues to rise. Numerous nuclear families live at some geographic distance from extended family, thus they may feel separated from their support system.

People continue to need the support only family can give. Recent studies show that individuals and nuclear families who are isolated from major support systems are more at risk of developing problems. Diana Garland, dean of the Baylor School of Social Work at Baylor University, provides a litany of problems that sometimes develop from isolation: "physical illness, suicide, psychiatric hospitalization, alcoholism, accident proneness, difficult pregnancies, depression, anxiety, child abuse, and family violence."[3] In other words, isolation contributes to the creation of family crisis. Isolation is either directly linked to causing the crisis, or it provides fertile ground for the development of a crisis.

Diana Garland calls for churches to have a ministry of nurture and support to families and to broaden their understanding of family to what she calls "ecological families." She defines an ecological family as "the relationships through which persons meet their needs for intimacy, sharing of resources, tangible and intangible help, commitment, responsibility, and meaningfulness over time and contexts."[4] David Garland calls for the church, as a family of faith, to fulfill this role "The church goes a long way toward Jesus' ideal that all persons will have brothers, sisters, and parents in God's family."[5]

All God's people need a family, and God's people need to strive to provide a family of faith to those in our world who are deprived of traditional family relationships. The church can initiate and nurture these essential, family-like relationships. We need to enhance our ministry of helping people discover family in the family of faith, moving our ministry with families beyond people who are already members. This ministry of helping families and individuals feel connected to others is important for families facing crisis.

As we reawaken Jesus' definition of family of faith, we also need to come to a new understanding of family. Whereas our society sees the home as a place of retreat, the New Testament presents a different picture of the home—a place of hospitality and service rather than retreat.[6] The challenge for churches is to help families see that they need to reach out in service to other families. After all, Jesus called us to be part of his family of faith not only for ourselves but for others.

RESPONSES OF THE CHURCH TO FAMILIES IN CRISIS

Garrison Keillor, the popular storyteller on a "Prairie Home Companion" and author of the book *Lake Wobegon Days*, used the provocative imagery of a storm home to describe the power of support. In his monologue, Keillor told how children from the countryside were assigned an in-town storm home. The storm home was a warm and inviting place for rural children to go in case a snowstorm prevented school buses from transporting them to their homes. Even though the boy in Keillor's story never had occasion to stay at his storm home, he imagined himself surrounded by caring people, waiting to provide him with love and hospitality. Knowing this resource was available to him gave him a powerful sense of security.[7]

The local church congregation becomes a storm home for families and individuals. People must perceive such churches as warm and inviting, safe, and resourceful. Families overwhelmed by a tragedy need to know that their church is an inviting place. Families also need the assurance that their church is a safe place that respects them and is prepared to deal with their life struggles. Churches, like storm homes, need to be resourceful. The storm home provides resources of food and shelter to meet the needs of the child unable to reach his or her home. Churches must grow in their ability to match their resources to the needs of families. As the family of God, the church, and individuals and families who make up the church, need to have a feeling of mutuality. Working together, we can find answers and share spiritual resources to help people arrive at workable solutions during times of crisis.

As churches nurture families who are already members and reach out to new individuals and families, families in crisis need particular attention. Where does a church start to help families, particularly those in crisis? Initially, churches must create programs that help people discover family. Many churches already provide events and activities such as fellowship meals, recreational programs, and discussion groups that foster the development of deeper relationships. Beyond this, a church's ministry to families in crisis has at least five components.

Crisis Intervention through Ministries of Care

When churches intervene to help families in crisis, they provide ministries of care. This dimension of the church's care includes but is not limited to the counseling and pastoral care provided by the pastor or other staff ministers. All Christians are God's ministers, but the paid ministers in most churches are particularly alert to families in crisis.

Churches have traditionally responded to some kinds of family crisis better than others. Pastors and laypeople alike generally respond in a variety of helpful ways to families suffering from grief over the death of a family member. However, churches are not as adept at ministering to families suffering from grief over the divorce of a couple. Churches need to be sensitive to the scope and variety of ways families experience crisis and reach out to provide a ministry of care.

Pastors and other staff ministers can lead the way in developing caring systems and programs to enhance the church's concern for families in crisis. One way of developing caring systems can be called the "committee method." Some churches use an organized system that meets a variety of family crisis needs. For example, many churches assign every church member to a deacon or other caring person to be their minister. This person is then responsible for maintaining contact with assigned families and providing caring visits in times of crisis. One church I served as pastor had several ministry teams responsible for ministry to families and individuals during specific and significant transitional periods as well as during acute crises. These ministry teams included the following:

• New Baby: Provide care and celebrate the birth of a new baby.
• Nursing Home: Regularly visit and minister to those in a nursing home.
• Homebound: Provide regular visits and ministry to homebound individuals.
• Hospital: Make regular visits and minister to the hospitalized and their families.
• Bereavement: Provide a ministry of care to families of the bereaved (including food as well as visits).

These, of course, can be expanded to cover a broader area of needs.

It was impossible for me, as pastor, to provide all the needed care to families and individuals in crisis. Through this network of ministry teams, the caring systems were active in order to serve a greater number of those in need. More than a visit from the pastor, families in crisis received support and encouragement from a member of their church family.

In addition to teams providing care to families in crisis, churches contain untold numbers of informal relationships. Silent and unassuming caring people do much of the church's ministry to families in crisis. Most congregations have a great army of people who counsel with their peers, offering hope and encouragement. Many of these silent caregivers have walked the same path of grief, divorce, or adjustment. I have observed, on more than one occasion, divorcees reaching out to minister to others who recently faced this situation. One lady who lost a child to cancer was sensitive and proficient in providing a ministry to the terminally ill and their families. Pastors and other church staff ministers can enhance the church's ministry to families in crisis by identifying and training these natural caregivers.

Both professional and lay caregivers need to be aware of some of the dangers involved in caring for others. Carmen Renee Berry reminds us in her book, *When Helping You Is Hurting Me,* that people's motives for helping others vary. Sometimes individuals get caught in what she calls a "Messiah trap." These Messiahs neglect themselves because they feel that they are supposed to sacrifice their own well-being for the sake of others. The "Messiah" may take extreme responsibility for the hurts of others, thus feeling indispensable. On the other side, the "Messiah" may feel as though he must earn his worth through his care for others and thus gets so busy taking care of others that he doesn't take care of himself. Or, as Berry puts it, "The Messiah trap is an odd combination of feeling grandiose yet worthless, of being needed and yet abandoned, of playing God while groveling."[8]

Those who provide care for families in crisis need to be aware that their worth is not tied to their caregiving. Their care for families in crisis should not cause them to neglect their care for themselves or for their own families.

Other traps exist regarding helping people in crisis. Earlier in chapter 3, we talked about family triangles. Caregivers need to remain alert to the possibility of being trapped in a family triangle. In a helping triangle, the rescuer often becomes the victim. For example, consider what sometimes occurs when a caring person reach out to help a couple having marital difficulty. In many cases, the helper hears only one side of the problem. While desiring to be supportive, the helper can take the side of the person he or she is helping. If a separation later occurs, this helper could then be blamed for the marriage failure, or as is sometimes the case, the helper could become the new lover.

These cautions are not intended to discourage those who wish to help. Rather, they are mentioned to encourage the household of faith to provide the kind of ministry that truly helps and not the kind that becomes hurtful.

Educational Programs

The church has a responsibility to link hands with Christian families in teaching values to children, youth, and adults. We often expect the school system to provide all the education children need. In a similar way, families have sometimes given the church total responsibility for religious education. A better solution exists when the church and home join their efforts.

One area in which church and home can join hands is teaching values. When both institutions work together, values are reinforced. Churches need to take seriously the education of people regarding such issues as AIDS, alcohol use, racial prejudice, and responsibility for the earth's resources.

Another way the church can help families in crisis is by teaching them what to expect in the various life stages. When people know better what to expect in life, they meet life's circumstances with more confidence and potentially avoid a crisis. A class for teenagers that helps them with relational and communication skills might prevent some marital crises in the future.

Additionally, churches can offer education to families regarding specific crises families face. The variety of crises presented in chapter 1 may generate further discussion and help families know what to expect should one of these arise.

Enrichment Opportunities

Enrichment opportunities, while not designed as tools for crisis intervention, offer much help to families as they chart their course through the developmental stages and even as they face more acute family crises. Family enrichment helps prior to crisis, during crisis, and following crisis.

Enrichment opportunities help families *prior* to a crisis. Small group interaction and interaction with family members during an enrichment event strengthen relationships and family life. Strong families are able to face a crisis better and move beyond it quicker.

Enrichment experiences can also help family members cope *during* a crisis. This is particularly true when the crisis is developmental. Parents of teenagers may experience difficulty related to parenting adolescents. These parents might benefit from attending an enrichment event for parents of teens. The supportive atmosphere in such a group could offer assistance to chart their course through the stormy teen years.

Again, enrichment programs are not designed to meet the needs of families in crisis. For this reason, families experiencing extreme or acute crises should probably avoid enrichment events. It is difficult for us in the church to exclude someone from attending a particular event, so we need to be aware of the fact that many times families or individuals experiencing a crisis attend an enrichment program as a way of receiving help.

For example, a couple having marital difficulty may wish to attend a marriage enrichment retreat. The enrichment format may stir up additional conflict that is impossible to address in an enrichment setting. Leaders of such events must be sensitive to specific needs of participants. Referral to a qualified counselor may help those in acute crises further process the feelings and issues raised at the event. The best help someone may receive at an enrichment event might be the discovery that he or she needs additional professional help.

Enrichment opportunities have a positive effect *following* the family crisis. Even when the crisis has passed, those who experienced it need opportunities to process their pain. Enrichment opportunities provide support groups and also give opportunities to process feelings related to a crisis.

Enrichment opportunities can help after the crisis has passed and families have made adjustments. Part of the enrichment format allows for small group discussion as well as conversation with one's spouse or other family member. If enough time has passed and a family has returned to its normal routine, the enrichment format allows for further processing of the crisis and helps the couple or family move back into the mainstream of the church's activities.

Continuing Support through Support Groups

Support groups have sprung up for every conceivable area of crisis. For example, there are support groups for grief recovery, divorce recovery, families of AIDS victims, parents of teens, alcoholics, single parents and married couples, and on and on. Many communities have seen the formation of support groups for family members of those deployed to Iraq or Afghanistan. While it might be impossible for a church to offer every kind of support group, a church can respond to the specific needs of people in their area. Support groups are not meant to take the place of individual care, but they provide a place for people who have been in similar circumstances to share with each other.

I am involved periodically in leading short-term support groups for ministers and their spouses who have been terminated by their churches. These groups meet in a retreat setting over a three-day period. Most participants attend with some reluctance, wondering what they will find and whether or not they will be accepted or blamed. In virtually every case, each person finds a great source of strength from others in similar circumstances. Since I, as leader, have not experienced termination from a job, I am at a disadvantage. However, I help those in the group tell their story and share their hurts. The wives, particularly, find a great source of strength from other wives in attendance.

Support groups, whatever their focus, have several essential elements. To be most effective, a support group needs a *clearly stated purpose*. This will give direction to the group. A purpose statement gives the group a reason for being as well as an intended direction. Without a stated purpose, a support group has no reference point from which to judge its effectiveness.

Confidentiality is a second essential element of a support group. Participants must be able to trust one another with information they share about their lives. Trust grows slowly as members risk sharing sensitive matters. Group members are able to become more vulnerable with one another as the group handles information responsibly.

Members' *commitment* to the group is also essential. Two parts of this important element are attendance and participation. Self-revelation is difficult for some people, and therefore each group member's needs and level of openness should be respected. Each group member is accountable to the group for his or her attendance and openness to participate. Participation includes listening as well as sharing one's own story.

Fairness means giving each group member time to talk. It also means listening without interruption and taking each group member seriously, giving full attention to the person talking.

Support groups need a balance between *affirmation* and *honest feedback*. Listening and providing an appropriate response is part of what it means to affirm others. As group members provide objective feedback, they help others in the group gain a different perspective.

Finally, the group leader of a support group serves the role of *facilitator*. While the leader facilitates learning, he or she is not a teacher. A facilitator guides a process, provides a non-anxious presence, offers affirmation, and gives objective feedback.

Ministry Through Small Groups

In the book *Planting Missional Churches*, Ed Stetzer says, "Small-group organizations include cell groups, home groups, Sunday school classes, and other gatherings that promote relationships in the family of faith."[9]

Over the past thirty years, churches across the USA have expanded their small group ministries. Small groups provide opportunities to move beyond the individualistic mindset of our culture. Participants in church-based small groups often become "family" as individuals come together as followers of Christ. Many times members of church-based small groups report finding relational intimacy not possible in other places.

Stetzer writes, "Small-group ministry is essential to the health of any church."[10] I might add that being part of a small group has the potential of enhancing the emotional and spiritual health of its participants.

Members of one's small group can provide essential support during a crisis. David Buckner is the coordinator of small groups in his church, and he recently experienced a family crisis when his sister died. When asked how his small group helped him, he answered with one word: "Safety." He further explained, "If a small group is doing what it is supposed to do, it creates a safe place to share hurts and find love and support." David's small group became a place of sharing and finding support during his family's time of grief.

All God's people need a family, particularly a family of faith. These then are five components of a church's ministry to families in crisis:

1. Crisis Intervention through Ministries of Care
2. Educational Opportunities
3. Enrichment Opportunities
4. Support Groups
5. Small Groups

Personal Learning Activity

What are five components of a church's ministry to families in crisis? Write each one in the space provided and include an example of how your church fulfills (or could fulfill) each component.

1. _____

_____

2. _____

_____

3. _____

_____

4. _____

_____

5. _____

_____

WAYS OF HELPING FAMILIES IN CRISIS

The church, as the family of God, provides an extended family for families; it is a much-needed resource. As ministers, individual Christians reach out to families and family members in need, providing love and concern. It is often easier to ignore crises families face because of the cultural taboo associated with family problems. This taboo generally says, "Family problems are no one else's business, so we don't need to stick our nose where it doesn't belong." We often fail to reach out to families in crisis because we don't want to get involved. We also run from pain in other families because of the anxiety it causes us.

I'd like to suggest helpful ways Christians can reach out to families and individuals in crisis. We begin by being accessible and taking appropriate initiative toward individuals or families in crisis. We show genuine concern and act in a trustworthy manner. We provide a ministry of acceptance and warmth. Throughout the process of providing help, we listen intently, enabling the hurting person or family to sort through their situation.

Be Accessible and Take Appropriate Initiative

Caring people do not force themselves on others. Instead, they maintain an "available" posture. How approachable are you? It is important to be physically and emotionally accessible. We give signals—sometimes nonverbal and indirect, sometimes open and verbal—that let people know whether or not we wish to be bothered by their concerns. A first step toward helping families in crisis is to be aware of our feelings of availability and to communicate our desire to help.

Simply being accessible is not always enough. It is important at times to take appropriate initiative toward people in crisis. I recognize that some forms of initiative are not considered appropriate. Medical doctors, as a rule, don't make house calls. Imagine your physician calling you to make a home visit to check on your sprained ankle. What is true of the medical profession is not true for ministers, whether paid ministers or lay caregivers.

The family of faith does not need to wait for people in need to ask for help. It is okay, and indeed desirable, for those of the household of faith to take appropriate initiative toward families in crisis. Our reluctance to do so might reflect our own anxiety about the crisis. I've heard more than one person say, "What do I say to a person getting a divorce?" To say nothing may communicate a lack of concern. A simple statement reminding a person of your prayers is enough to open the door to provide additional ministry.

When I'm uncertain about specific needs, I often ask the person to suggest ways I can be of help.

We can take initiative in a variety of ways. Nothing can take the place of personal contact. A warm touch, combined with a verbal expression of concern, can be a powerful ministry. We can take appropriate initiative by inviting a hurting individual or family to our home for a meal, thus allowing our whole family to be involved in the ministry of hospitality. Following my accident as a teenager, I remember a kind church member visiting in our home and later taking us to a restaurant for a snack. I do not remember what words of encouragement he used, but his visit communicated a powerful message of concern. More than forty years later, I remember it.

Sometimes a home visit may be more of an inconvenience than a help. Families in crisis are already experiencing time pressures, and a visit might only add to their stress. We may use other means of taking initiative, such as a telephone call. A brief call to remind someone of our prayers and concern might give them a lift for the day. It might also open the door for a future, more intense ministry.

Whereas a home visit might have been appropriate in an agrarian society, in our technologically attuned world, an e-mail, text message, or message via Facebook may be more appropriate. Concerning use of the latter, unless a person has posted a public note concerning their crisis, it may be more appropriate to send a private note on Facebook than to post a message on their wall.

On some occasions, we might use the postal mail to take initiative. This can include sending a sympathy card as well as sending notes of concern at other times. A note could read, "I'm thinking of your family during this time," or "Our prayers are with you as you [make an important decision, cope with a particular difficulty, etc.]." This is an unobtrusive way of appropriately taking initiative. One particular occasion when a note, phone call, or e-mail is appreciated is near the anniversary of the death of a family member. The first anniversary of a death and the first Christmas holiday season following a death are particularly painful.

Show Genuine Concern

Our concern for others is based on God's concern shown in Jesus Christ. As servants of Christ, we look to him as our model. Paul reminds us in Romans 12:9, "Let love be genuine" (NRSV). Our love for families in need is based on God's love as fully expressed in Jesus Christ. Our love is sincere. We are enabled to express this kind of love through the power of the Holy Spirit and through our sensitivity to the needs of others.

We then become channels of Christ's concern, which we can express in multiple ways. We express our concern when we are accessible, take appropriate initiative, or pay attention. Another way of offering genuine concern is when we express empathy. When we do so, we feel with the other person by paying attention, listening, and providing encouragement.

The person who shows empathy "gets inside" the other person and looks at the world through that person's eyes. He or she has a sense of what the other person's world is like and communicates back to the other person this understanding and feeling. Carl Rogers, the father of client-centered therapy, says empathy is sensing the private world of another person as if it were your own, but without ever losing the "as if" quality.[11]

We show that we are genuinely concerned when we listen to a person describe her hurts. At times we may listen passively as a person gets something off his chest. These occasions of passive listening while someone tells a story or vents feelings may be all the person needs.

On other occasions we may engage in what is called active listening. In these conversations, we listen for both information and feelings. As we assess someone's situation, we might then mirror back feelings that, in turn, may provide an opening for the sharing of even deeper feelings.

The act of listening has a mysterious power to provide healing. I'm not suggesting that simply hearing someone out will solve his or her problems. However, as we listen to people pour out their souls, they sometimes rid themselves of negative feelings that they might otherwise turn inward.

Paul suggests in Romans 12:15 that we "Rejoice with those who rejoice, weep with those who weep" (NRSV). As members of the family of faith, we rejoice with individuals and families, celebrating their successes and important events. On other occasions we express our genuine concern as families struggle and undergo crises. Our sensitivity to people's needs become a channel of Christ's concern.

Be Worthy of Trust

People who care can be trusted to handle relationships and information with integrity. Those who hear family problems can be trusted to avoid gossiping. Trust increases when words match deeds. Caring persons who develop trusting relationships consistently practice what they claim.

Trust is broken when words and deeds don't match. Examples abound in the business world. When the quality of goods and services does not match the claims of advertising, trust erodes. Caring people must take care to follow through with claims they make.

Trust is built over time. As individuals prove trustworthy with small concerns, people begin to trust them with larger issues. Hear the words of Jesus: "Whoever is faithful in a very little is faithful also in much; and whoever is dishonest in a very little is dishonest also in much" (Luke 16:10, NRSV). I have observed that people often tell me small problems as a way of assessing my trustworthiness to hear larger problems.

Trust is built as caring people act with competence. Churches need to offer training opportunities for those desiring to provide ministries of care.

Offer Warm Acceptance

Warmth and acceptance are two sides of the same coin. This includes relating to others in a warm manner and accepting them where they are. All people need acceptance. The books most often stolen from the New York system of public libraries are those about etiquette. That's no surprise since such books tell what is socially acceptable and unacceptable. People crave acceptance because rejection is devastating.

Paul said in Romans 15:7, "Welcome one another, therefore, just as Christ has welcomed you, for the glory of God" (NRSV). Paul was talking about hospitality, but that's not all. Paul was also talking about the twin traits of acceptance and warmth. People who desire to provide a ministry to individuals and families in crisis are able to accept them and relate warmly in spite of their faults and failures.

Caring people are not afraid of taking the lead in being friendly and relating in a warm manner toward others. At times this might simply mean speaking to someone first. It includes not being aloof or arrogant in the manner of relating. It might also mean not walking away from a conversation but allowing enough silence for someone to express a need or issue.

People who care accept others without condoning immoral or unethical behavior. This means accepting others without being judgmental. The experience of Jesus with the woman at the well is an excellent example. He challenged her lifestyle while communicating his acceptance of her as a person of worth. Jesus valued the person without condoning her sinful actions. We become channels of God's grace as we accept others as people of worth, created in God's image.

Personal Learning Activity

List four ways you, as an individual, can help families who are experiencing a crisis.

1. _____

_____

2. _____

_____

3. _____

_____

4. _____

_____

SUMMARY

We began this chapter with the statement that every family needs a family, particularly a family of faith. This is because so many families and individuals currently experience isolation from traditional systems of support. Isolation contributes to the development of family crises.

Jesus redefines family and challenges churches to reach out to include people in the family of faith. We looked at five ways churches can do this:

1. Crisis Intervention through Ministries of Care
2. Educational Opportunities
3. Enrichment Opportunities
4. Support Groups
5. Small Groups

In the last section we discussed ways caring individuals can help families in crisis:

1. Be accessible and take appropriate initiative.
2. Show genuine concern.
3. Be trustworthy.
4. Show warmth and acceptance.

NOTES

1. M. John Lepper Jr., "Enriching Families in Your Church," *The Quarterly Review* (October 1990): 5.

2. Diana S. Richmond Garland and Diane Pancoast, eds., *The Church's Ministry with Families: A Practical Guide* (Dallas: Word Publishing, 1990) 28.

3. Ibid., 15.

4. Ibid., 11.

5. Ibid., 33.

6. Ibid., 32.

7. Quoted in Ted Bowman, *Methods and Materials* (July 1990): 35.

8. Carmen Renee Berry, *When Helping You Is Hurting Me* (New York: Harper and Row, 1988) 7, 10.

9. Ed Stetzer, *Planting Missional Churches* (Nashville: Broadman & Holman Publishers, 2006) 207.

10. Ibid.

11. Carl Rogers, "The Necessary and Sufficient Conditions of Therapeutic Personality Change," *Journal of Consulting Psychology* 23 (Spring 1978): 168–77.

LIVING WITH AN AMENDED FUTURE

A crisis brings lasting change. Like it or not, our future is amended by a crisis. I was reminded of this fact some time ago when Dr. William Marshall, then executive director of the Kentucky Baptist Convention, spoke to the staff. He became chief executive when the convention's resources were at a peak. When Dr. Marshall talked to the staff, he pointed out that the high plans and dreams held at the beginning were amended to match the reduction of resources.

In much the same way, families begin with high hopes and dreams. Most newlywed couples have unusually high hopes and dreams, never considering the trouble that will befall them in the coming years. But somewhere along the way, dreams are amended as crisis comes home.

What is true for families and organizations is sometimes true for a nation. This was the case for the Israelites who were taken as captives to Babylon. We find their feelings about their amended future in Psalm 137. Their captors asked them to sing a song of Zion. Psalm 137:4 expresses their deep hurt: "How could we sing the LORD's song in a foreign land?" (NRSV).

Families today may have a similar response when crisis changes their circumstances. At times we don't feel like singing at all. On other occasions we are able to sing, but only through our tears. We may ask, "How can our family ever sing the Lord's song again?" But the darkness changes to dawning and we can once again sing songs of joy. The day comes when hope, which once seemed only a flickering light, shines brightly again.

I've mentioned the experience of Victor Frankl, the Austrian psychiatrist who was imprisoned in Hitler's concentration camps and later developed logotherapy. In the closing of his book, *Man's Search for Meaning*, Frankl talks about the suffering of prisoners of war and how life would be for those who were liberated.

> But for every one of the liberated prisoners, the day comes when, looking back on his camp experiences, he can no longer understand how he endured it all. As the day of his liberation eventually came, when everything seemed to him like a beautiful dream, so also the day comes when all his camp experiences seem to him nothing but a nightmare.

The crowning experience of all, for the homecoming man, is the wonderful feeling that, after all he has suffered, there is nothing he need fear any more—except his God."[1]

Maybe to a lesser degree, but no less real, families who have experienced crises can respond in like manner. One day you will look back on your family crisis and wonder how you endured it all. But as the day of your liberation eventually comes—when you finally move beyond your nightmare to your dream—you are able to reflect on God's presence and power that enabled your family to grow in the process. Your anxieties about life have diminished. Your faith in God has been restored or deepened. You have grown as a person, and you can say, with Frankl's "homecoming man," that after all your family has suffered, there is nothing you need fear anymore. The God revealed in Jesus Christ has walked with your family through this crisis. God promises to walk with you into the future. You are, indeed, able to sing the Lord's song in the strange land of change!

NOTE
1. Victor E. Frankl, *Man's Search for Meaning* (New York: Pocket Books, 1973) 148.

A TEACHING MODEL

This teaching model is a group leader's plan for the book *When Crisis Comes Home.* This workshop, as well as the book, accepts the fact that every family at one time or another faces a crisis situation. Realistic suggestions are made that help participants prepare for, deal with, and learn from personal and family crisis. The group leader will find specific suggestions of how he or she can guide participants along the journey toward becoming equipped to respond to a family crisis. (This teaching model originally appeared in *Journal of Family Ministry* 8/1 [1994].)

INTRODUCTORY MATTERS

Experiential in nature, this model is based on the belief that learning is best reinforced when people interact with the information and feelings contained in the content. For this reason, the person who uses this plan is both a teacher and a group facilitator, one who imparts knowledge and also guides the process of learning. As presented, the model is about four hours in length. It can easily be expanded to six hours or condensed to two hours.

While this teaching plan contains some of the book's content, the leader should read the book in order to interpret and understand the flow of the material and have a more thorough knowledge of the nature of family crisis.

PREPARING TO LEAD

Gather the following items: pencils, blank paper, cards for the introductory exercise, a chart pad, worksheets as noted, and several copies of the book *When Crisis Comes Home.* (Ideally, each participant should have a copy.) Information for the worksheets is provided at the end of this appendix. For good group discussion, it is best to hold the workshop in an open room with chairs arranged in circles or around tables for small group interaction (5 to 8 people per group).

Begin by suggesting that crisis is something all families experience at one time or another. Suggest that some portions of the workshop might become emotionally heavy, but assure your group that you are going to have as much fun with crisis as possible. Further suggest that you will begin on a light note by asking them to listen and respond to a story you will read. Divide the participants into groups, giving each group a card with the following words:

1. DANGERS (What dangers are present for this crew?)
2. OPPORTUNITIES (What positive opportunities exist for the crew?)
3. FEELINGS (What might the crew be feeling now?)
4. CHALLENGES (What challenges does this crew face?)

Depending on the number of people present, you may give more than one group the same assignment, or you may combine numbers 2 and 4, "opportunities and challenges."

Say, "I'm going to read a true story. Your group will be asked to discuss your subject and the question on your card. This is an adaptation of a true story that appeared in *Sail* in October 1992. I'll read this story in three phases, stopping after each section to give you an opportunity for discussion within small groups then hear reports from groups."

Now read the following, allowing time for your groups to complete the instructions after each phase.

Phase One: The month is April, but it is the beginning of winter because we are in New Zealand in the Southern Hemisphere. Four men set sail from Picton, on New Zealand's South Island, to Tonga, about 1,500 miles to the north. They are an experienced crew, sailing aboard a 41-foot cruising trimaran. It's a beautiful day for sailing.
Instructions: With what you know, talk about your assigned subject with your small group. Address your subject and the question on your card.

Phase Two: John, the skipper, built this boat to be unsinkable. Having cruised the Pacific with his brother, he has 40,000 miles under his keel, so to speak. Phil calls another boat his home, where he lives with his wife and two children. Rick, an ex-cop and ex-Outward Bound instructor, was diagnosed with terminal cancer three years earlier. James, the only American aboard, is also the only non-sailor.

Four days out from New Zealand, the winds begin to pick up. As they increase, stormy weather seems to be on the horizon.
Instructions: With what you know, talk about your assigned subject. Address your subject and the question on your card.

Phase Three: The stormy weather is actually a gale. The boat capsizes, turning completely upside down. The main hull is half-filled with frigid 55-degree water. The crew huddles in what was the aft cabin, scarcely the size of a double bunk. As hope of rescue ebbs, their survival seems impossible. Instructions: With what you know, talk about your assigned subject. Address your subject and the question on your card.

After hearing the reports, your group will want to know what happened to the crew. The crew survived. They lived on the upside-down boat for 119 days. The men avoided starvation by rationing the few provisions aboard and catching an occasional fish. The boat drifted to an island, where it broke apart as it washed ashore.

The application of the exercise relates to the Chinese symbol for the word "crisis." Actually, it is made up of two Chinese symbols, one meaning danger and the other meaning opportunity.

For further application, mention that on any Saturday in June, a young and beautiful bride and a handsome groom say their vows, begin a family, and sail away. It's a beautiful day for sailing! Then one day the cool breezes become stronger and storm clouds appear on the horizon.

Danger and opportunity are always present for families. It's difficult to see danger on sunny, breezy days; it's difficult to see opportunities on stormy days. Staying together and growing together are opportunities and challenges for families. Capsizing or breaking apart can also be the result. The latter is more likely to occur when families are overwhelmed by the dangers and unable to see the challenges and opportunities.

Ask the small groups to think about opportunities/challenges families face as crisis comes home. These may include staying together, growing together, making it beyond the crisis to joy, peace, and harmony.

Ask the small groups to think about dangers families face as crisis comes home. These may include capsizing, further tragedy, breaking apart, nobody rescuing them.

Present a mini lecture based on the kinds of crises families face (see chapter 1). Crisis comes home to families in various ways. Two basic categories of crisis are *acute* and *developmental.* An acute crisis is sharp and intense, while a developmental crisis may be less intense and last for a longer period of time. The first chapter also outlines two other ways contemporary families experience crises. These are related to or brought about by *social or natural disasters* and by *trends in society.*

Use worksheet #1 (see below) as a way to help participants identify and begin to talk about a family crisis. This worksheet can unleash deep emotions, some of which may have been denied or repressed for a long time. Be prepared to coach the small groups on ways they can hear and encourage one another. Allow time for groups to discuss the information and answers given on the worksheet.

HOW FAMILIES FUNCTION

Divide the group into five smaller groups, assigning each group one of the ways families function (chapter 3). Ask them to read and discuss this section. Ask each group to appoint a spokesperson who will make a two- to three-minute report to the large group on the assigned subject.

Chapter 3 discusses five general characteristics of how families function. A summary is presented here to aid you in organizing your lesson plan:

1. Move toward balance.
2. Develop rules.
3. Develop hierarchies.
4. Develop triangles.
5. Develop a closeness/distance barometer.

Families, by nature, move toward *balance*. When a family member becomes ill, gets in trouble, or has something traumatic occur, the whole family is brought off balance. Immediately, other family members compensate in order to help the family system regain its balance. This homeostatic balance occurs in both healthy and unhealthy ways. For example, one family member may cover for an addicted family member. This keeps the family in balance but may also enable the sick family member to stay addicted.

Families develop *rules*. Whether written, spoken, secret, or in the open, families live by rules. These rules govern behavior and relationships of family members. Rules are important to the daily routine of families because they help the members know acceptable and unacceptable behavior. A crisis interrupts or disrupts the rules.

Families develop *hierarchies*. Structures of authority help families make decisions and accomplish tasks. In this way, chaos and unpredictability are avoided. Some families have a rigid power structure, while other families have a more free-flowing power system. Generally, the norm for families is for the older generation to have authority over the younger. Healthy families exhibit a flexible kind of leadership.

Families tend to develop *triangles.* An emotional triangle is any three-way relationship. It can include people and issues and often evolves as a way of coping with stress. When tension in a family system increases, another person or issue is sometimes pulled into the relationship. When this occurs, an emotional triangle is formed that temporarily eases or absorbs stress in family relationships. In the long run, however, triangles serve to increase family problems.

Families develop a particular *closeness/distance* norm. What is "normal" for one family might be abnormal for another. Some families are close and dependent while others are distant. A middle ground seems to characterize healthy families. Excessive distance or excessive closeness can intensify an existing crisis or even cause a crisis. Extremely close families may, of necessity, blow apart during difficulty. Distant families are not much better because family members are cut off from emotional support.

RESPONDING TO A CRISIS

Explain that this understanding of how families function will help us in learning how families respond to a crisis. Hand out worksheet #2 (see below) and ask participants to jot notes and complete it as you discuss ways families respond to crisis.

Crisis brings changes. The most pervasive effect of a crisis on families is change. Life is full of changes, but crisis hastens the process of change. Depending on the situation, change may be short lived or long term. Developmental crises bring changes at a more relaxed pace, while acute crises bring immediate changes. Crises related to disaster or societal kinds of crises may bring both immediate and long-lasting changes. In any case, a family crisis brings changes in roles, responsibilities, and, sometimes, lifestyles.

Crisis disrupts family routine. When families experience a crisis, the family's routine is disrupted. Families in crisis often feel like they are living life on hold. The disruption that takes place during an acute crisis may be more intense during certain phases of the crisis.

Crisis limits control. A crisis leaves families, to one degree or another, out of control. A crisis causes us to lose control over people, relationships, and events. It's as if the crisis controls our lives. Life must go on and daily choices must be made, but the crisis often governs our decisions.

Crisis alters communication patterns. Increased stress brought about by a crisis brings a change in the way a family communicates. A certain family member may normally be the communication link for the whole family. If this person is incapacitated, communication must find a new channel.

Families often have unspoken rules about how and even whether information is shared with other family members. Under normal circumstances and concerning most subjects, a family might be open with one another. A crisis forces a family to decide how to handle certain information.

Poor communication further adds to a family's inability to grow through a crisis. Families with poor communication patterns are in danger of regressing as a result of a crisis.

Crisis causes time pressure and increased fatigue. A crisis intensifies a family's time. The crisis may consume so much time that normal family obligations are neglected.

Fatigue is a natural consequence of time pressure. Family members often go without sleep in order to care for others. Because the crisis stimulates bodily functions, families in crisis often initially respond with superhuman strength. But the stimulation wears thin rather soon, and fatigue becomes the order of the day for families in crisis.

Allow time for the group to complete worksheet #2, and then ask them to turn to a neighbor and discuss the information on the sheet. Process with the large group by asking for a few brief examples or responses.

Next, take about ten minutes to discuss negative ways families respond to a crisis (see chapter 3):

• rigidity
• prohibition against sharing feelings
• denial
• poor communication
• blaming
• physical violence
• substance abuse

PRESCRIPTION FOR FAMILIES FACING CRISIS

Hand out worksheet #3 (see below), and ask participants to jot notes about what is said and how their families have experienced each area that is discussed. Also ask them to think of ways they might improve each area. (See chapter 4 for a full discussion.)

Rx 1: *Pull together.* Families are better able to face a crisis if they are already accustomed to pulling together as a family. Pulling together takes a great deal of willingness on the part of family members. Each member must have a desire to work together. As family members willingly share household and family responsibilities, the whole family is better able to grow through the crisis.

Rx 2: *Encourage clear and open communication.* Families are better able to pull together if their communication patterns are positive and helpful. Good communication includes sharing information as well as feelings. Families whose communication is so characterized find themselves in a better position to solve problems related to a crisis. Open and clear communication increases problem-solving effectiveness.

Rx 3: *Go with the flow. Practice flexibility.* Tall pine trees in Florida seldom break in the winds because they have the unique ability to bend and sway. Their durability comes partly from their flexibility. Another characteristic of a palm tree is resilience. Even after being blown about by strong winds, the trees keep uprighting themselves; they keep bouncing back.

Families are able to withstand the storms of life, in part, because of their flexibility and their resilience.

Rx 4: *Use resources wisely.* A family's ability to seek valuable support from others helps them cope with a crisis. It is a mark of health for a family to recognize the need for outside help and reach for it.

Rx 5: *Draw on spiritual resources.* This includes the matters we generally think of as spiritual resources such as faith in God, strength from God's word, strength from the power of the Holy Spirit, strength from Christian friends, and strength from the church.

Explain that more will be said later about spiritual resources. Ask your participants to review the worksheet and place a check mark beside two of these that they consider strong in their families. Place an "X" by two that need more work. Allow time for them to discuss this in their small groups or with a neighbor. Also allow time for several people to share insights they gained related to the worksheet.

Spiritual Resources

The prophet Isaiah said, "But those who wait for the LORD shall renew their strength, they shall mount up with wings like eagles, they shall run and not be weary, they shall walk and not faint" (Isa 40:31, NRSV). Notice that one admonition is to wait. Our haste to find a quick answer sometimes limits God's ability to exercise power. The word "renew" in this verse literally means "to exchange." The sense is that we exchange our weakness for God's strength.

Review briefly seven ways families can draw on spiritual resources. These are discussed in chapter 5 and include the following:

1. Nurture faith in God.
2. Cultivate the fruit of the Spirit (Gal 5:22-23).
3. Strive for congruence, genuineness, integrity.
4. Practice church involvement.
5. Use teachable moments.
6. Take time to laugh.
7. Claim the blessing.

Tell the group you would like them to focus on cultivating the fruit of the Spirit as an important spiritual resource. Point out that studies have shown that a key ingredient in healthy, strong families is "spiritual wellness." The elements of the fruit of the Spirit are marks of spiritual wellness. Ask group members to read Galatians 5:22-23 and think about how each element of the fruit of the Spirit helps families cope during a crisis. Assign one or two of these per group; ask them to discuss how their assigned "fruit" helps families cope during a crisis. Allow five minutes for small group discussion, and then ask for reports from the groups.

WAYS CHURCHES CAN RESPOND TO FAMILIES IN CRISIS

Divide the group into four smaller groups. Briefly review with them the section in the book that describes four ways churches can respond to families in crisis (chapter 6). These are

1. crisis intervention through ministries of care.
2. educational programs.
3. enrichment opportunities.
4. continuing support through support groups.

Ask each smaller group to read the section in the book assigned to them and be prepared to describe their topic to the larger group. Give each group a large piece of chart paper or newsprint and ask them to write their topic at the top and take notes on the sheet as they brainstorm ways this is working or might work in their church. Allow ten minutes for small group discussion, and then hear reports from each group.

WAYS INDIVIDUALS CAN PROVIDE CARE

Give a mini lecture on ways individuals can provide care to others in crisis. Caring people are accessible and take appropriate initiative. They do not force themselves on others; however, they are approachable and have an available posture. Caring people show genuine concern for others in crisis. They are worthy of trust. People who care can be trusted to handle relationships and information with integrity. Warm acceptance is an important attribute of a caring person. This involves relating to others in a warm manner and accepting them where they are.

CLOSURE

Hand out blank sheets of paper and ask participants to write down a couple of things they have learned in this workshop that will help them better face a crisis. Then ask them to write one way they hope to help others in a crisis. Ask for several people to share insights, observations, or commitments. Conclude with a challenge for participants to reach out to families and individuals who face a crisis.

Worksheet #1
NAMING THE CRISIS

1. Name the crisis. Write a word or phrase that describes a crisis your family has experienced or is currently experiencing. If you experienced several crises simultaneously, include each of these in your description.

_____

_____

_____

_____

2. Name the category (or categories) of the crisis (acute, developmental, social, disaster-related).

_____

_____

_____

_____

3. Name the feelings related to this crisis or these crises.

_____

_____

_____

_____

4. Name the dangers related to this crisis or these crises.

_____

_____

_____

_____

5. Name the opportunities or challenges related to this crisis or these crises.

_____

_____

_____

_____

Worksheet #2

RESPONDING TO A CRISIS

Being aware of typical responses to crisis helps us better understand and deal with what our family is going through. Place a check mark by the characteristics that describe how a particular crisis has affected your family.

_____ Brought changes in roles, responsibilities, and lifestyles.

_____ Disrupted our family routine.

_____ Caused us to lose control over people, relationships, and/or events.

_____ Altered communication patterns around our house.

_____ Caused us to experience time pressures and increased fatigue.

Worksheet #3

PRESCRIPTION FOR FAMILIES FACING CRISES

Rx 1: *Pull together.*
Description—

_____

Ways your family pulls together—

_____

Rx 2: *Encourage open and clear communication.*
Description—

_____

Examples of open and clear communication in your family—

_____

Rx 3: *Go with the flow.*
Description—

_____

Ways your family is flexible—

_____

Rx 4: *Use Resources wisely.*
Description—

_____

Who would provide support for your family if a major crisis occurred?

_____

Rx 5: *Draw on spiritual resources.*
Description—

_____

How have you experienced the value of spiritual resources in your family?

_____

Breinigsville, PA USA
23 September 2009
224649BV00003B/1/P